NAVIGATING CAREER ROADMAPS

Developing Your Professional GPS through Internships

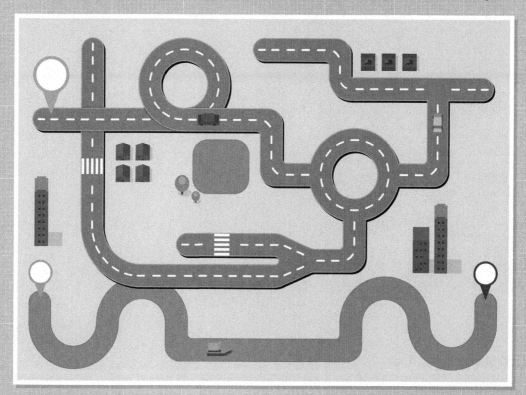

Jennifer L. Gonyea
Melissa Scott Kozak

Kendall Hunt
p u b l i s h i n g c o m p a n y

Kendall Hunt
publishing company

www.kendallhunt.com
Send all inquiries to:
4050 Westmark Drive
Dubuque, IA 52004-1840

Contents

1 Where Are You Coming From?

OBJECTIVES

By the end of this chapter you should be able to:

➤ Reflect on your personal, professional and civic identities
➤ Identify current time management strategies and techniques to improve
➤ Identify your biases
➤ Differentiate between strengths-based and deficit perspectives

PERSONAL IDENTITY

As instructors who work with undergraduates, we observe our students struggling to identify who they are as Human Development and Family Studies/Science students and how best to use their knowledge and skills. Many of them speak passionately about "working with people," but they have difficulty articulating what that actually means with regards to their future, and how "helping people" may be a deficit-based perspective. It is important that students learn how to identify and understand the needs of the communities and individuals they are working with, instead of assuming that they know what others want (Ballard & Carroll, 2005; Bringle & Hatcher, 2002; Lanigan, 2008; Sandy & Holland, 2006). Before you can understand others, you have to understand yourself.

Who are you? When, and with whom? Identity is complex and, depending on the time and place, could be defined in multiple ways. As a student, you are developing your identities: personal, professional and civic. But what do those mean? One way to explore your personal identity is through a Life Map activity (Hall, 2010). The purpose of this activity is to visually represent your life from birth to the present time in order to identify how you have been impacted by people and places, as well as how you have impacted others. To complete your Life Map, please refer to the *Applying Your Knowledge* section of this chapter.

WHERE DOES THE TIME GO?

Think about your daily routines—what do you do when you wake up in the morning or before you go to sleep at night? Daily routines play an important role in your identity because they reflect your values. For example, how you spend your time and whom you interact with illustrate what and who you think are valuable. Also, these routines play an important role in how your body and mind function. If unhealthy routines develop, you are more susceptible to stress, and who needs that?

To begin thinking about self-care and reducing your stress, identify what your daily routines are for 168 hours, or one week. You can find the activity in the *Applying Your Knowledge* section of this chapter. Effective time management, which you will need in your internship and professional environments, includes knowing how you spend your time and where you can 'borrow' time when needed. This will enable you to be productive and fully engaged with yourself, your peers, your clients and the community.

You should consistently review your daily routines. What do you spend the most and the least amount of time doing? In many cases, there are activities that are considered "time suckers." These activities take up a good amount of our days, but by opting to do them we become ineffective and waste our time. According to your routines, what are your time suckers? What do they prevent you from doing? Do they add or take away from your stress? How can you change your routines today to remove the time suckers and stressful experiences? On a piece of paper, a computer or your hand, write at least 5 things that you can do and how you will hold yourself accountable.

It is important to assess what strategies you use to manage your time. For example, is procrastination a tool you utilize? How many times have you told yourself that you produce better work under pressure? Or, are you just busy and have a lot of things on your plate? You can find comfort knowing that you are not alone. Procrastination is an issue that many people face, but researchers now distinguish between those who procrastinate, and those who are procrastinators. The difference being that someone who procrastinates may use it as a strategy sometimes, while procrastinators have difficulty with emotions, like self-regulation (Jaffe, 2013). Time management is a process and a journey that evolves over time and it depends on many factors. However, there are some basic skills that can help build a solid foundation for success that can be adapted to fit your life.

You began your journey by assessing how you currently use your time. The next step is to understand your processes better. *Psychology Today* (2011) offers a "Time Management Skills Test"[1] to determine whether or not you stay one step ahead, or whether you are constantly procrastinating. What did you discover from the test about your skills? What do the results say about your ability to manage your time?

---

[1]You can take the test here: http://psychologytoday.tests.psychtests.com/take_test.php?idRegTest=3208

Once you identify skills you could improve upon, you can begin to identify strategies to turn those weaknesses into strengths. A contributor to *Business Insider,* Jacquelyn Smith (2014) described *12 Things Successful People do In the First Hour of the Workday*[2]. They are:

1. Reflection
2. Strategize
3. Review to-do lists and calendars
4. Update to-do lists and calendars
5. Plan for the time consuming projects
6. Avoid conflict or conflict resolution with others
7. Write with purpose
8. Interact with others positively
9. Briefly review emails
10. Stay focused
11. Avoid meetings
12. Relax

In recent years, many articles have been circulated about how creative people spend their time, providing evidence for our desire to learn what works, or to justify our less-than-stellar ability to manage our time. In a nutshell, individuals from Benjamin Franklin to Sigmund Freud have had diverse time management skills, but the one thing consistent across all creative individuals explored was a routine.

To help you identify some tools or applications to help you manage your time and develop a routine, here a few resources that we have found helpful.

1. Teux-Deux.com
2. Google Calendar
3. One Note
4. Remember the Milk
5. Mindmeister
6. List.ly
7. Evernote

To understand the role of stress in your life, complete the *Inventory of College Students' Recent Life Experiences (IC-SRLE)* (Kohn, Lafreniere & Gurevich, 1990). The ICS-RLE was developed as a valid and reliable tool to enable students to understand not only what stressors are there in their lives, but also how often they experience them. You can find the activity in the *Applying Your Knowledge* section of this chapter.

Stress impacts our ability to function every day, and influences your cognitive, physical and socioemotional development (Kohn, Lafreniere & Gurevich, 1990). Each individual experiences stress differently, so it is important to understand the source of your stress, as you determined with the ICSRLE Survey. As you analyze your results, recognize that stress can be both positive and negative; it is really all in

[2]Read more: http://www.businessinsider.com/how-successful-people-spend-their-first-hour-at-work-2014-3#ixzz35rVcFYh2

how you approach it. If you have the perspective that the glass is half-full, stress can be an opportunity for growth and change. Stressed is desserts spelled backwards!

At this point in your life, it is important to create routines and patterns that allow you to work on achieving a school, life balance that is appropriate for you. Balance looks different for everyone and changes across the life course. Although your life experiences may change, the strategies that you develop now can be adapted to fit the situation. Understand your reactions to stress and shift your focus. For example, if you procrastinate when you experience stress, then develop a list of tasks that will help you stay accountable. Or, take some deep breathes and move your body. No one can tell you *the one* magic solution that will help you manage your stress. It is your responsibility to determine what works best for you, in your situation. If you do find that your inability to manage stress is impacting your life in negative ways, such as school work or relationships, we encourage you to use community resources. Contact the Student Support Services Office at your university, or the campus counseling center.

PROFESSIONAL IDENTITY

What Do You See?

Explore the image and write down everything you see. After you record your observations, what do you think about the situation depicted in the image?

How the personal affects the professional

Who do you want to be seen as a professional? Think about the personal identity exercises you completed and determine where your interests are in the world. How does your daily routine reflect your personal values? What target population, age, place, or circumstances do you want to explore?

To further delve into how your personal identity impacts your professional one, you can explore your professional interests by using an Intergenerational Model (Anderson & Sabatelli, 2011) to look at patterns that have influenced your professional interests and potential career trajectory.

Step 1: Create a three generation Intergenerational Model.
Step 2: Label the professions and educational levels of each member.
Step 3: Look for occupational patterns among generations.
Step 4: Reflect on how these patterns have positively or negatively impacted your own career interests. For example, have you rejected occupations in the criminal justice field because your parents were police officers or lawyers?

You can also assess your biases using Project Implicit (2011)[3]. Select a test of your choice (e.g. Religion, Sex/Gender, Sexual orientation, Income level/SES, Immigrant status, etc.). Think about the results and if you think they are accurate. It is important to assess your personal biases before entering an internship because you will interact with supervisors, colleagues and clients who are different from you in multiple ways.

Because of the diversity that exists, using a strengths-based perspective is useful. According to Green, McAllister and Tarte (2004), there are 10 important factors to consider:

1. Empower individuals by building on their strengths. This also involves meeting them where they are and not forcing them to meet where you are.
2. Have cultural competence and understand individuals' beliefs
3. Develop an appropriate and supportive relationship
4. Help individuals and families identify and develop supportive relationships
5. Become a partner
6. Understand the history of the community
7. Identify resources in the community
8. Use a family-centered approach
9. Understand how to set appropriate short and long term goals for yourself and others
10. Understand how to individualize experiences—one size does not fit all

Before working with others, identifying your own strengths and weaknesses can be beneficial. Take a moment and list 10 of your strengths. Now, identify 10 weaknesses. Review each list and identify how your weaknesses can be strengthened. Find a method that works for you and record how you will accomplish your goals. Keep it close and work on it regularly. For some, sharing it with a friend or family member can provide helpful accountability.

To understand and utilize the factors above, you must be open to challenging your perspective and experiences. It is one thing to assume that you know what people need, but it is another thing altogether to ask them what they need. Consider the following scenario based on a student's internship experience.

Imagine that you are working with a mother who was referred to a social services agency because she abused her daughter. In her file, you read that the abuse that occurred was spanking and that this

[3]https://implicit.harvard.edu/implicit/takeatest.html

caused frequent bruises and marks on her daughter's backside. After a few sessions, the mother continues to disagree with you every time you say that she abused her daughter. Getting nowhere, you finally ask her, "Why is it not abuse?" The mother responds, "Because my father abused me, and what I am doing is not the same." After further encouragement, she continues to describe the lasting marks that she has from being burned, cut and being subjected to other methods of physical abuse. She explains, "The marks I leave on my daughter go away; mine will last forever. I am *not* abusing her." By asking questions, you met the mother where she was, not where you needed her to be. If you hadn't taken the time to understand her, the sessions would not have progressed.

How could you continue to work with this mother and help her understand why spanking her daughter is abuse? Perhaps you can ask the mother, "Are there marks that he left that went away?" If she responds yes, then you have helped her make the connection. Additionally, ask the mother how she would describe her father. Then ask her, "If I asked your daughter to talk about how she feels when you spank her, or after, what do you think she would say?"

Within this story, we also discover how to be culturally competent by recognizing that our experiences are not our clients' (Neukrug & Milliken, 2008). Part of personal and professional growth is actually investing in it. As a student, you must take it seriously and identify how your beliefs, values, biases, etc. could impact relationships between you and your future clients (Neukrug & Milliken, 2008). In the above scenario, the key to success was creating an open environment with the mother so that she felt safe in sharing her story. Instead of judging her for not understanding that she was abusing her child, the student recognized that there were other important factors at play. To work effectively in the field, you must be willing to recognize how social institutions have influenced you, those with whom you work, as well as the work that happens in the field itself. We will explore this further later in the chapter in regards to dual relationships and professional boundaries.

In this scenario, using a strengths-based perspective enables you, your colleagues and your families to be empowered, because weaknesses are not the focus. Instead, you identify strengths that can help improve the weaknesses. This can be difficult for anyone, but especially new professionals. In the United States, culturally we are made to believe in individuality and independence. We are taught the golden rule: treat others as you would like to be treated. However, what if your values do not match those of the people you interact with on a regular basis? Popularized after a *How I Met Your Mother* episode, the platinum rule states, "Treat others as they would like to be treated" (Thomas & Bays, 2007). This represents a strengths-based perspective because it moves away from an ethnocentric perspective that puts your ideals and beliefs above all others. Ethnocentrism is a culture-specific view that can deleteriously influence your ability to look beyond your beliefs and judge others by assuming that their beliefs are harmful or wrong (Rogoff, 2003).

In the human services field, it is important to understand that normality is culturally dependent (Neukrug & Milliken, 2008). As individuals, we must be "willing to obtain knowledge about all diverse groups" (Neukrug & Milliken, 2008, p. 19). Now that you've explored how your personal and professional identities interact, you can become more aware of how your personal biases (from Project Implicit (2011) results) impact how you interact with others and make value-based judgments about their behavior. You can use this information to identify why individuals you work with react differently than you do, or resist help from an organization that you would like to learn more about.

Explore the image again and write down everything you see. After you record your new observations, what do you think now about the situation depicted in the image?

CIVIC IDENTITY

Review your Life Map Activity again and identify what elements of yourself portray you as a community member.

Questions to Consider

In which communities are you a member?

How does your identity change depending on the community you are in; what role you play in those communities; how and why?

What groups do you belong to (race, ethnicity, gender, class)?

Are you privileged?

Do these connect to or challenge your professional goals?

As you wrestle with your identities, experiential learning opportunities like internships can integrate you into a community and learn more about yourself. Internships facilitate the intersection of your personal identity and academic knowledge, which enables you to understand who you are within the community context and develop professional skills (Embersole & Worster, 2007).

Place-based education (Green, 2007) is about an educational experience that is "holistic, integrated, and meaningful, thereby facilitating the development of… [their] knowledge, skills, and dispositions towards the local culture," or community (Embersole & Worster, 2007, p. 20). In place-based internships, you learn contextual information about the environment or circumstance, e.g. SES, neighborhood safety, family structure; these types of internships provide an opportunity for you to understand and potentially become part of a new community, or redefine your role within it. You can become more invested in your community and gain cultural competency, which will allow you to continuously think critically and reflexively on your clients' personal identities, and the identity of the community where they are learning and experiencing the world. Before you know it, you are a social steward who is civically engaged in your community.

Although you are on the periphery of your professional identity, you become more civically minded and engaged as you work directly with individuals or agencies. You may have received information about career options in the classroom, but you may still feel unsure of exactly what the day-to-day responsibilities are of professionals working in the human services field, for example, therapists, Family Life Educators, caseworkers, or advocates. Your internship may stimulate new goals for your future, or help to identify strengths that you have that will enable you to contribute in the community (Ballard & Carroll, 2005; Prouty, Johnson & Protinsky, 2000). In later chapters, we will discuss how to gain more awareness of your internship community.

Before you get there, work on increasing your cultural competency now by doing something different. Select a time frame (a day, week, or month) and plan what you will do differently based on your existing routine. Change your diet, transportation, use of electronics, or place of worship. As you do something different, keep a diary each day and record your assumptions before you change, as well as your experiences after. *What did you learn?* This exercise is important because, as human beings, we are routine-oriented, which often means we self-select people and environments that make us feel comfortable. However, we therefore do not challenge ourselves or our perspectives in doing so. Take a chance.

Once you take a chance, revise your Life Map. Each new, relevant experience should be included to accurately reflect who you are and why. We are always learning more about ourselves, others and our environment.

FEELING THE STRAIN: MANAGING THE TRANSITION FROM BEING A STUDENT TO AN INTERN

In the human services field, self-care is crucial. If you are unhealthy or unable to care for yourself first, you will be a less effective professional (Turner, et al., 2005). In addition to the *normal* demands of your life (as you discovered above), internships include additional stressors that impact your ability to function in your personal, professional and civic spheres. For some students, it will be difficult to adjust to a new schedule that may involve course work, employment, or a sole focus on the internship. For other students, the content of their internship will be difficult to handle. You may work with families whose parental rights are terminated, or with adults who have severe developmental delays. Professionals in the human services field are at a higher risk of being affected by depression, stress and emotional exhaustion (Turner et al., 2005), which makes it that much more important that you consciously think about your personal self-care. Regardless of the situation, adjustment will occur and you will be responsible for developing ways to manage your self-care.

One way to identify a self-care strategy is by reviewing the activities that decrease your stress. It may be finding a hobby, routine, friends or media outlet that help you unwind at the end of the day and perhaps even recharge your energy. As discussed earlier, using a strengths-based perspective is helpful for clients, but it can also be helpful for you. As Turner et al. (2005) found, instead of focusing on the negatives in your internship, focus on the positives and the coping strategies you know are effective.

Because you may revise your strategies over time, you should also discuss them with your supervisor and internship colleagues. As seasoned professionals, ask them what they do personally or organizationally to de-stress (Turner et al., 2005).

Reassessing the Status Quo

When you begin an internship or transition into the workforce, you will encounter a lot of changes that will undoubtedly cause you to refocus your energies in the face of stress. To combat stress most effectively, you need to reevaluate what aspects of your life are particularly stressful, as well as how stressed you are this very moment. To do this, you will complete the Inventory of College Students' Recent Life Experiences (ICSRLE) (Kohn, Lafreniere & Gurevich, 1990) again. Do not worry; a second copy is included in the *Applying Your Knowledge* section.

INTERN IDENTITY

At this point, you are no doubt thinking about what a daunting task your internship will be. Good! While you are in your internship, focus on the inquiry aspect of learning. You are being thoughtful about where you see your future—if you make the internship about inquiry (confirming or disconfirming your path), then the choice is yours. There is value in understanding that you've chosen where you are going and you are empowered to forge

Find your passion!

your own way (Gilardi & Lozza, 2009). As an intern, it is your responsibility to work on "positive attitudes, sensitivity to diversity, and increasing confidence in facilitating hands-on science participation, inquiry, and collaborative work" (Katz et al., 2010, p. 1169).

According to Lave & Wenger (1998), interns engage in legitimate peripheral participation. In other words, as an intern you are at the periphery of your eventual professional community. You are not yet fully skilled; therefore you learn from professors and then your supervisors in the community and develop attitudes by observing how the professional community acts. This acculturation into your professional identity through the accumulation of skills and attitudes occurs as you engage with your professional community and the community in general, and through observing role models in both university and internship placements. In this way, you are also developing a mentor relationship with your supervisor that will help you understand even more about the processes of working in the field (Von Dras & Miller, 2002).

A difficult component of your role as an intern is maintaining professional boundaries with supervisors, colleagues and clients. In the Human Services field, this research is grounded in the Social Work field, and dual relationships are discussed often and relate to our previous discussion of meeting clients where they are. Findings suggest that students report after internships how important it is to balance life and work, and also comment about the need to put the client first and address their needs professionally, and not act based on what you observe or think they need (Diambra, Cole-Zakrzewski & Zakrzweks, 2004). This can be difficult because many students believe that in the classroom they are told to maintain a distance with future clients. However, once they begin to work with clients in their internships, they learn that they must develop relationships to earn respect (Alexander & Charles, 2009). To address this, it is important that your roles as an intern are clearly defined in the classroom and in the field (Mc-Clam, Diambra, Burton, Fuss & Fudge, 2008). In later chapters, we will discuss specific methods to do this, which include making educated decisions informed by national standards and the ethical principles defined by a national organization, such as the National Council on Family Relations (NCFR).

Now is a good time to revisit time management. Review your time log activity and identify who you interact with and where on a weekly basis. Identify themes that are present; for example, do you frequently go to the same places or see the same people? Why? If someone else were to look at how you spend your work/school time, what would they think is valuable to you? Does that reflect what you really think is important? If not, how can you restructure your time to reflect what is important to you? Now do the same thing for your personal or discretionary time.

LIFE MAP

To create your map, use pictures, narratives or other relevant symbols and documents that provide evidence of your identity. Tangible evidence is needed for this activity because it is one thing to think that you are who you are, but it is another to find documentation that supports the way that you think.

Step 1: Before you begin, answer the following questions.

1. What is your sex and gender identity? How has this impacted your life (e.g. extracurricular activities, friends, academics, life goals, etc.)?

2. When did someone impact you significantly?

3. When did you impact someone significantly?

4. What are your strengths and weaknesses? How have they changed?

5. How have parents, friends, family impacted you?

6. How has the media impacted you?

7. Are there particularly positive or negative experiences that have impacted you? Why?

Step 2: Gather crayons, magazine clippings, photos, or other representative symbols to create your Life Map.

Step 3: Life experiences, such as the ones suggested by the guiding questions above, play a role in your development as a person and shape the way you see yourself, the world around you, and how you interact with others. Now that you have a visualization of your identity, reflect on the following questions.

1. What aspects are most important to you? Why?

2. How do your personal characteristics impact your professional identity and decisions?

168 Hours Exercise

The following activity was developed by Michigan Tech University (2014) and will help you identify your time use patterns.

Starting when you leave class, and for the next week track all of your activities large and small. Each hour is split into 30 minute increments to make tracking smaller time commitments easier Round up or down as you see appropriate. If you would like to use an alternate tracking method, please feel free BUT you must tally you various activities to receive full credit for this assignment.

TO TALLY: You must add up the time you spent doing certain activities. Some like: Sleeping, Eating, Personal Hygiene, Class, and Studying should be applicable to all. Others like Work or Varsity Sports Practice are specific to the individual, but not any less time consuming. Look at where your time goes, if you are spending multiple hours a week on something, it probably deserves its own category (For example, if you go mountain biking or have bible study 6 hours a week it is a significant time commitment).

Smaller tasks that are a part of the same thing may be combined if you wish (For example, if you spend 2 hours on laundry and 1-1/2 hours cleaning and organizing your living space you could combine it into one category called "housekeeping"). You may tally on the bottom of this sheet or on separate sheet.

Word of advice: the more specifics you have, the more helpful this assignment this is. So, combining everything that doesn't fall into a Sleeping, Eating, Class, Work, or Studying category as "free time," or creating some other broad category like "socializing" is not particularly beneficial; although, you are organize things however they make sense to you. You will find there is a difference between the time you spend spending an extra 45 minutes talking in the dining hall versus participating in something planned like a student organization meeting or University event.

Your totals should add up to 168 hours.

168 Hours Assignment

	WED	THURS	FRI	SAT	SUN	MON	TUES	WED
12:00 AM								
1:00 AM								
2:00 AM								
3:00 AM								
4:00 AM								
5:00 AM								
6:00 AM								
7:00 AM								
8:00 AM								
9:00 AM								
10:00 AM								
11:00 AM								
12:00 PM								
1:00 PM								
2:00 PM								
3:00 PM								
4:00 PM								
5:00 PM								
6:00 PM								
7:00 PM								
8:00 PM								
9:00 PM								
10:00 PM								
11:00 PM								

THE INVENTORY OF COLLEGE STUDENTS' RECENT LIFE EXPERIENCES

The following is a list of experiences which many students have some time or other. Please indicate for each experience how much it has been a part of your life *over the past month*. Put a "1" in the space provided next to an experience if it was *not at all part* of your life over the past month (e.g., "trouble with mother in law- 1"); "2" for an experience which was *only slightly* part of your life over that time; "3" for an experience which was *distinctly* part of your life; and "4" for an experience which was *very much* part of your life over the past month.

Intensity of Experience over the Past Month

0 = not at all part of my life
1 = only slightly part of my life

2 = distinctly part of my life
3 = very much part of my life

_____ 1. Conflicts with boyfriend's/girlfriend's/spouse's family
_____ 2. Being let down or disappointed by friends
_____ 3. Conflict with professor(s)
_____ 4. Social rejection
_____ 5. Too many things to do at once
_____ 6. Being taken for granted
_____ 7. Financial conflicts with family members
_____ 8. Having your trust betrayed by a friend
_____ 9. Separation from people you care about
_____ 10. Having your contributions overlooked
_____ 11. Struggling to meet your own academic standards
_____ 12. Being taken advantage of
_____ 13. Not enough leisure time
_____ 14. Struggling to meet the academic standards of others
_____ 15. A lot of responsibilities
_____ 16. Dissatisfaction with school
_____ 17. Decisions about intimate relationship(s)
_____ 18. Not enough time to meet your obligations
_____ 19. Dissatisfaction with your mathematical ability
_____ 20. Important decisions about your future career
_____ 21. Financial burdens
_____ 22. Dissatisfaction with your reading ability
_____ 23. Important decisions about your education
_____ 24. Loneliness
_____ 25. Lower grades than you hoped for
_____ 26. Conflict with teaching assistant(s)
_____ 27. Not enough time for sleep
_____ 28. Conflicts with your family
_____ 29. Heavy demands from extracurricular activities
_____ 30. Finding courses too demanding
_____ 31. Conflicts with friends
_____ 32. Hard effort to get ahead
_____ 33. Poor health of a friend
_____ 34. Disliking your studies
_____ 35. Getting "ripped off" or cheated in the purchase of services
_____ 36. Social conflicts over smoking
_____ 37. Difficulties with transportation

____ 38. Disliking fellow student(s)
____ 39. Conflicts with boyfriend/girlfriend/spouse
____ 40. Dissatisfaction with your ability at written expression
____ 41. Interruptions of your school work
____ 42. Social isolation
____ 43. Long waits to get service (e.g., at banks, stores, etc.)
____ 44. Being ignored
____ 45. Dissatisfaction with your physical appearance
____ 46. Finding course(s) uninteresting
____ 47. Gossip concerning someone you care about
____ 48. Failing to get expected job
____ 49. Dissatisfaction with your athletic skills

(Kohn, Lafreniere & Gurevich, 1990)

Add up your total to determine how stressed out you are; the higher the number, the more stress you are experiencing. Now, identify the items above with the highest numbers, these are your biggest stressors. With these two takeaways, what steps can you take to reduce your stress?

THE INVENTORY OF COLLEGE STUDENTS' RECENT LIFE EXPERIENCES

The following is a list of experiences which many students have some time or other. Please indicate for each experience how much it has been a part of your life *over the past month*. Put a "1" in the space provided next to an experience if it was *not at all part* of your life over the past month (e.g., "trouble with mother in law- 1"); "2" for an experience which was *only slightly* part of your life over that time; "3" for an experience which was *distinctly* part of your life; and "4" for an experience which was *very much* part of your life over the past month.

Intensity of Experience over the Past Month

0 = not at all part of my life
1 = only slightly part of my life

2 = distinctly part of my life
3 = very much part of my life

_____ 1. Conflicts with boyfriend's/girlfriend's/spouse's family
_____ 2. Being let down or disappointed by friends
_____ 3. Conflict with professor(s)
_____ 4. Social rejection
_____ 5. Too many things to do at once
_____ 6. Being taken for granted
_____ 7. Financial conflicts with family members
_____ 8. Having your trust betrayed by a friend
_____ 9. Separation from people you care about
_____ 10. Having your contributions overlooked
_____ 11. Struggling to meet your own academic standards
_____ 12. Being taken advantage of
_____ 13. Not enough leisure time
_____ 14. Struggling to meet the academic standards of others
_____ 15. A lot of responsibilities
_____ 16. Dissatisfaction with school
_____ 17. Decisions about intimate relationship(s)
_____ 18. Not enough time to meet your obligations
_____ 19. Dissatisfaction with your mathematical ability
_____ 20. Important decisions about your future career
_____ 21. Financial burdens
_____ 22. Dissatisfaction with your reading ability
_____ 23. Important decisions about your education
_____ 24. Loneliness
_____ 25. Lower grades than you hoped for
_____ 26. Conflict with teaching assistant(s)
_____ 27. Not enough time for sleep
_____ 28. Conflicts with your family
_____ 29. Heavy demands from extracurricular activities
_____ 30. Finding courses too demanding
_____ 31. Conflicts with friends
_____ 32. Hard effort to get ahead
_____ 33. Poor health of a friend
_____ 34. Disliking your studies
_____ 35. Getting "ripped off" or cheated in the purchase of services
_____ 36. Social conflicts over smoking
_____ 37. Difficulties with transportation
_____ 38. Disliking fellow student(s)

_____ 39. Conflicts with boyfriend/girlfriend/spouse
_____ 40. Dissatisfaction with your ability at written expression
_____ 41. Interruptions of your school work
_____ 42. Social isolation
_____ 43. Long waits to get service (e.g., at banks, stores, etc.)
_____ 44. Being ignored
_____ 45. Dissatisfaction with your physical appearance
_____ 46. Finding course(s) uninteresting
_____ 47. Gossip concerning someone you care about
_____ 48. Failing to get expected job
_____ 49. Dissatisfaction with your athletic skills

(Kohn, Lafreniere & Gurevich, 1990)

Add up your total to determine how stressed out you are; the higher the number, the more stress you are experiencing. Now, identify the items above with the highest numbers, these are your biggest stressors.

With these two takeaways, what steps can you take to reduce your stress?

REFERENCES

Alexander, C. & Charles, G. (2009). Caring, mutuality and reciprocity in social worker client relationships: Rethinking principles of practice. *Journal of Social Work, 9*(5), 5–22. doi: 10.1177/1468017308098420

Anderson, S. A. & Sabatelli, R. M. (2010). *Family Interaction: A Multigenerational evelopmental Perspective, 5th Ed.* Boston: Allyn and Bacon.

Ballard, S. M., & Carroll, E. B. (2005). Internship practices in family studies programs. *Journal of Family and Consumer Sciences, 97*(4), 11–17.

Diambra, J.F., Cole-Zakrzewski, K.G., & Zakrzweks, R.F. (2004). Key lessons learned during initial internship: Student perspectives. *Human Service Education, 24*(1), 5–18.

Ebersole, M., and Worster, A. (2007). Sense of place in teacher preparation courses: Place based and standardsbased education. *The Delta Gamma Bulletin 73*(2): 19–24

Gilardi, S., & Lozza, E. (2009). Inquiry-based learning and undergraduates' professional identity development: Assessment of a field research-based course. *Innovative Higher Education, 34,* 245–256. doi 10.1007/s10755-009-9109-0

Green, B., McAllister, C, & Tarte, J. (2004). The strengths-based practices inventory: A tool for measuring strengths-based service delivery in early childhood and family support programs. *Families in Society, 85*(3), 326–334.

Hall, M. (2010). Life map activity. In *Readings for diversity and social justice* (Chapter 1). Retrieved from http://cw.routledge.com/textbooks/readingsfordiversity/section3/ch-01-c.pdf

Katz P, McGinnis JR, Hestness E, Riedinger K, Marbach-Ad G, Dai A, Pease R (2011) Professional identity development of teacher candidates participating in an informal science education internship: a focus on drawings as evidence. *International Journal of Science Education, 33*(9):1169–1197. doi:10.1080/09500693.2010.489928

Kohn, P. M., Lafreniere, K., & Gurevich, M. (1990). The inventory of college students' recent life experiences: A decontaminated hassles scale for a special population. *Journal of Behavioral Medicine, 13*(6), 619–630.

Lave, J. and Wenger, E. (1998). *Communities of practice: Learning, meaning, and identity.* Cambridge, UK: Cambridge University Press.

McClam, T., Diambra, J. F, Burton, B., Fuss, A., & Fudge, D. L. (2008). An analysis of a service-learning project: Students' expectations, concerns, and reflections. *Journal of Experiential Education, 30*(3), 236–249.

Michigan Tech University. 168 Hours Exercise.

Neukrug, E. & Milliken, T.F. (2008). Activites to enhance the cultural compentence of human services students. *Human Services Education, 28*(1), 17–28.

Project Implicit. (2011). Retrieved from https://implicit.harvard.edu/implicit/takeatest.html

Prouty, A. M., Johnson, S., & Protinsky, H. O. (2000). Recruiting the next generation of marriage and family therapists through undergraduate internships. *Journal of Marital and Family Therapy, 26*(1), 47–50.

Psychology Today (2011). *Time Management Skills Test.* Retrieved from: http://psychologytoday.tests.psychtests.com/take_test.php?idRegTest=3208

R.J. (2014, March 26). *Creative Routines.* Retrieved from http://infowetrust.com/2014/03/26/creative-routines/

Rogoff, B. (2003). *The cultural nature of human development.* New York: Oxford University Press.

Smith, J. (2014, March 19). *12 Things Successful People Do In The First Hour Of The Workday.* Retrieved from http://www.businessinsider.com/how-successful-people-spend-their-first-hour-at-work-2014-3#ixzz35rqRkNDu

Thomas, C. & Bays, C. (Writers), & Fryman, P. (Director). (December 10, 2007). The Platinum Rule [Television series episode]. In Hseuh, B., Kang, K., & Mamman-Greenberg, S. (Producers), *How I met your mother.* Los Angeles, CA: 20th Century Fox.

Turner, J.A., Edwards, L.M., Eicken, I.M., Yokoyama, K., Castra, J.R., & Tran, A.N. (2005). Intern self-care: An Exploratory study into strategy use and effectiveness. *Professional Psychology: Research and Practice, 36*(6), 674–680. doi: 10.1037/0735-7028.36.6.674

Von Dras, D. D., & Miller, K. M. (2002). Learning outside of the classroom: The undergraduate gerontology internship. *Educational Gerontology, 28,* 881–894. doi: 10.1080=03601270290099877

Would You Hire Your Digital Self?

OBJECTIVES

➤ Describe the ways organizations use digital identities to screen for potential employees
➤ Evaluate your own digital identity
➤ Create a strategy to improve a digital identity
➤ Identify ways to minimize negative information on the internet

Fast forward a semester or so. At that point, you will have completed your internship, evaluated your personal and career goals, researched job opportunities that would meet both of these, contacted the organizations, and interviewed at your top choices. Say you are lucky (and well-prepared) enough to get a great offer from one of your top choices. Good job! In your excitement about landing your first job offer, you send a Tweet saying, "[company name] just offered me a job! Now I have to weigh the utility of a fatty paycheck against the [long] daily commute and hating the work." Unfortunately, you didn't check the privacy box, and the Twitterverse, including the company you reference, now has access to your comment.

Connor Riley (aka Cisco Fatty; Popkin, 2009) found out the hard way how blurred the lines between work and personal life can become when she wrote the Tweet mentioned above. Someone claiming to be an associate for Cisco, the company Riley refers to, replied that she would be happy to forward the Tweet to the Cisco hiring manager. Urban legend has it that the job offer was rescinded although Riley states that the offer was for an internship that she had already turned down (Popkin, 2009).

"NICE TO VIRTUALLY MEET YOU"

As many as 60% of American corporations monitor their employee's use of social media sites such as Facebook, YouTube, and LinkedIn (Gross, 2012). Some companies have employees whose sole job is to monitor the Internet for references to the company for brand management and marketing purposes or to research potential employees via social media.

According to CareerBuilder (PRNewswire, 2012), 37% of the 2000 hiring managers surveyed reported using social media to research job candidates, with an additional 11% planning to start this practice. Companies who currently use social media as a screening tool for potential employees are looking for the applicant's professionalism, whether or not they are a good fit for the company, and/or additional evidence of the applicant's qualifications. Some companies are even possibly looking for reasons *not* to hire the candidate and statistics show that they were more likely to find that type of information (34%) than they were to find information that helped make the decision to hire the applicant (29%; Careerbuilder, 2012). Table 2.1 lists the prevalence of the reasons why applicants were or were not hired based on their social media posts.

Unfortunately, your first impression to potential employers is no longer when you shake their hand at the start of the interview. Your *digital identity* consists of your online reputation represented by all media types across the social web and is often your first impression to an internship site or a potential employer.

TABLE 2.1. Percentages of hiring managers reports of information that influenced hiring decisions. (Created using information from CareerBuilder, 2012)

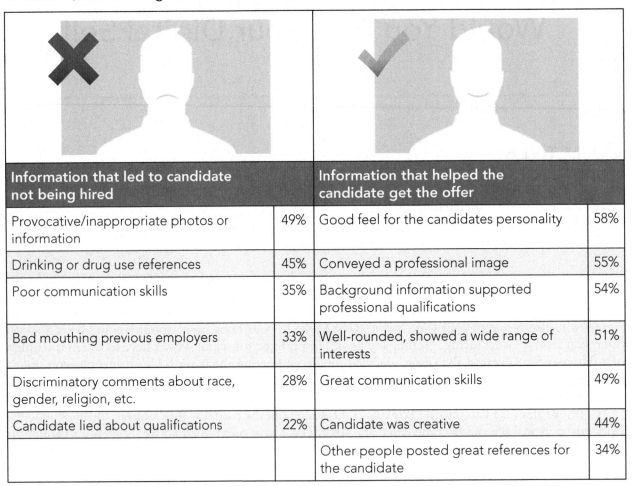

Information that led to candidate not being hired		Information that helped the candidate get the offer	
Provocative/inappropriate photos or information	49%	Good feel for the candidates personality	58%
Drinking or drug use references	45%	Conveyed a professional image	55%
Poor communication skills	35%	Background information supported professional qualifications	54%
Bad mouthing previous employers	33%	Well-rounded, showed a wide range of interests	51%
Discriminatory comments about race, gender, religion, etc.	28%	Great communication skills	49%
Candidate lied about qualifications	22%	Candidate was creative	44%
		Other people posted great references for the candidate	34%

The healthcare, education, and business fields have paid the most attention to the impact of digital identity on professionalism and the ability to be successful. Family Science graduates have a lot in common with these three other disciplines. First, healthcare and education programs prepare students to become service providers, working directly with individuals and families. As such, professionals in all three of these fields represent their profession and their discipline to the community—even when they are not at work—making it imperative that they maintain sufficient boundaries in their public digital presence. Second, all three of these professional fields require some degree of confidentiality in handling consumer information. Professionals in the healthcare and education fields are taught and reminded not to have conversations with their coworkers in public spaces, such as the hallway, the elevator, or the cafeteria, due to the possibility of being overheard. The elevator of the new millennium is social media (Mostaghimi & Crotty, 2011). Lastly, graduates of business schools understand the importance of managing your brand in order to foster trustworthiness in your consumers. Family Science graduates similarly rely on their reputation because of the nature of the content and the ways in which they interact with individuals, families, and the community.

Students appear to be aware of the way their identity in the community and their professional identity are related, but are unaware of the impact this can have on their careers. For example, an overwhelming majority of students (88%) agree with the statement that their behaviors outside of a clinical environment impact their ability to do their jobs (Garner & O'Sullivan, 2010). Despite this, a significant proportion of students (46%) also felt that what happens on social media is somehow separate from what happens in their life at college (Garner & O'Sullivan, 2010). So, why is there such a disconnect between how we perceive our digital lives and our brick and mortar lives? It becomes even more complicated when we consider that over half of these same students reported that there were photos of themselves they found embarrassing online and that they saw unprofessional behavior on the part of their colleagues, based on photos of excessive drinking, various states of undress, and content related to inappropriate boundaries about the workplace (Garner & O'Sullivan, 2010). Internship placements and potential employers have access to these embarrassing photos that document unprofessional behaviors, because 96% of the students sampled had their social media accounts in the same name that they use professionally.

In a recent study of medical students' use of social media and the influence of their social media use on their professional life, one participant summed the relationship up nicely, "God, you're just judged all the time" (Finn, Garner, & Sawdon, 2010, p. 819). Though it's frustrating to think this way and the student's statement appears to be a complaint, being constantly evaluated is a reality in the digital age. As a student, an intern, a job candidate, a new employee, or just someone who has a digital identity, your decisions, actions, performance, and very self are being judged by others who may or may not know you personally.

Some students in Garner and O'Sullivan's (2010) study expressed that their personal life, as it is documented on Facebook, was unrelated to their career. Though everyone is entitled to his or her opinion, in this case your opinion about the separation between your personal life and your professional life has less impact than the opinion of those in decision-making positions. For example, internship coordinators, supervisors, employers, stakeholders, consumers, and the community at large have the final say in how your personal and digital life relates to your professional life, through their ability to open or close doors to internship possibilities, making hiring decisions, and in some cases making firing decisions (See inset).

Social media posts cost them their jobs

1. Ashley Johnson was fired from her waitressing job for using the company's name when she complained about two customers who left her a bad tip after making her stay late.
2. A British woman was dismissed from a jury for polling her friends about which verdict to she should support.
3. Caitlin Davis, an NFL cheerleader, was fired for being shown in a picture with a marker and a passed-out woman with swastikas and "I'm a Jew" written on her.
4. A Swiss woman was fired for using Facebook on a day she called in sick, stating that she had a migraine and that she needed to be in a darkened room.
5. Hospital staff in England were suspended for posting pictures of themselves playing the "Lying Down on the Job Game" and lying down in various places in the hospital.
6. Andrew Kurtz was fired for making negative comments about the owners and manager of the Pittsburgh Pirates, the team for whom he was a pierogi mascot.

7.   13 Virgin Airlines flight attendants who posted details about the passengers were fired.

8.   A teacher from Charlotte, NC was fired for posting that she worked in "the most ghetto school in Charlotte."

9.   A Buckingham Palace Guardsman was fired for calling Kate Middleton names on his Facebook page.

10. A Bronx high school teacher was fired for commenting "This is sexy" on pictures his students shared.

11. Ashley Payne was fired from her high school teaching position for posting a picture of herself holding a glass of wine while on vacation on her Facebook page.

12. Nathalie Blanchard was collecting disability benefits for depression, which she promptly lost because her Facebook page contained pictures of her vacationing on the beach, at a Chippendale's-type club, and generally not appearing very depressed.

13. A British woman was fired for calling her boss a 'pervvy wanker' and saying she hates her job.

14. The day after a student died on the class beach trip, Christine Rubino posted that she wouldn't throw a student a life preserver for a million dollars. She was fired and is fighting for her job back.

15. A Spanish nun was asked to leave her convent for being on Facebook too much.

16. Tania Dickinson was fired for calling herself a "very expensive paperweight" who was "highly competent in time-wastage, blame-shifting, and stationary theft."

17. Frank Samuelson was fired from his little league coaching position in Georgia for making racist comments on his Facebook page.

Adapted from Love, D. (2011). 17 People who were fired for using Facebook. The Business Insider. Retrieved from http://www.businessinsider.com/facebook-fired-2011-5?op=1

Building a Professional Digital Identity

It seems as though the message in the information presented thus far is that you can't post anything about your personal life on social media. You can't be human, make an error in judgment, or just plain have a bad day—at least not publicly. This presents a serious challenge for the current generation of college students, interns, and soon-to-be graduates who are firmly entrenched in the digital age. One might say this generation has grown up online and, as a result, may not even be aware of the potential ramifications of their social media persona.

The solution to the blurred boundaries between personal and professional is to separate the two digital identities from one another. Finn, Garner, and Sawdon (2010) suggest developing two gears: one directed toward consumers and professional peers (professional digital identity) and one directed toward peers who are student peers and/or friends. Students and interns face an additional challenge of being engaged in identity negotiation (Finn, Garner, & Sawdon, 2010). Thus, they haven't yet developed a professional identity, and therefore the *only* digital identity they've constructed revolves around their personal and private lives.

Students are confused about where and when they need to be aware of professionalism and to what degree. For example, what type of professionalism is required of students and interns, who are clearly still learning the culture of their chosen profession? What should be the appropriate consequences of a lack of professionalism, given that supervisors and employers can't expect interns to have had the exposure to professional acculturation that employees are likely to have had? This leads to the questions of what is required of a 'professional' versus a student, and how interns can learn the difference.

An excellent way to think about the importance of how you present yourself in your digital identity is in regard to how you dress. Most students know that they should dress in professional attire, be well-groomed, and use their best professional manners when interviewing in person for their internship. Similarly, most interns know that they should wear different clothes at their internship site than they would ordinarily wear to attend class. But, the question remains: how does your professional self *dress* in your digital identity? Your 'professional' attire for your digital self consists of all the pieces of information about who you are as a professional that are available online. For example, your connections to other professionals, other community members, professional associations, your own postings, pictures, likes, and subscriptions create your digital professional identity.

Your internship is a great time to start building your professional wardrobe, so to speak, or building your digital professional identity. As you prepare to engage in your community through an internship, you can start building the foundation of your professional digital identity by creating new accounts on social media. Use these new accounts to build your professional network as you interview for internships, engage with community organizations, and other professionals in your community with whom you share similar career interests. Make sure that you keep these accounts separate from your personal accounts. Also, keep your professional accounts public and your personal accounts protected with the highest degrees of privacy settings. Though it is still possible for some of your personal to become public, it will reduce the likelihood of blurring your personal and professional selves online. Another advantage is that your professional digital identity will have more public activity and in some ways bury the personal activity below your professional activity. This will thereby prime any searches about you with the information about your professional activities rather than your personal ones, and potentially decrease the likelihood that the personal ones will even be seen.

Use these new accounts to document the ways you are engaging with your community and your profession through your internship experience. Since you may not have a lot of professional experience, you can fill out your new professional identity with documentation of your internship through blogging about your experiences and the skills you are building in the process; just be mindful of confidentiality. Another option is to document progress on projects you complete as a part of your internship; for example, posting promotional materials for a program you are developing or documenting your participation in community work group. In the final chapter, we will discuss how to build your LinkedIn Profile to include these experiences.

As you take part in your professional community in person, you should use your professional accounts to engage in websites that are related to professional interests such as community agencies, advocacy groups, professional organizations, relevant non-profits, among others. Notice that campus groups and resources are not included in this list of professional sites. By associating your professional digital identity with professional and community organizations and omitting campus ones, you are beginning to send a subtle message about your evolution from student to employee through your ability to leave the familiar (campus) and enter into the professional world. Lastly, your new professional accounts should only be used to connect with people who are professionally relevant. In other words, keep your friends, family, roommates, and significant others for your personal, private social media accounts.

Another way to increase the visibility of your professional profile online is to have a short biography that briefly summarizes your resume or curriculum vitae, specifically your experience, skills, and any niche areas in which you have particular expertise. Closing old accounts that are no longer relevant to your personal or your professional identity can further push your professional profiles higher in a search related to your name. Also, make certain your accounts use your professional moniker and not one that is cute, immature, or even a reference to your alma mater – no matter how loyal a fan you are! Finally, critically assess your newly created social media accounts using the perspective of a potential employer. We encourage you to complete the Your Digital Identity activity in the (italicize) Applying Your Knowledge section of the this chapter.

SUGGESTIONS FOR MANAGING VIRTUAL IDENTITY

Once you've established a professional digital identity, you can begin to promote yourself for an internship continuing to build your professional digital identity through your applied experience to promote yourself for a job. Consider yourself a small business and promote your knowledge and experiences as the services your small business offers.

Using guidance from home business entrepreneurs, you can build your professional digital identity by following basic guidelines. Daniel Burrus (2011), a leading technology forecaster, offers the following nine guidelines for promoting yourself through social media.

1. Use your social media accounts to build trust. As an individual marketing yourself for an internship and/or a job, this translates to building your expertise in a particular area. You need to convince the reader or viewer that you are knowledgeable in your particular area and provide evidence of this knowledge.

2. Be transparent about your identity and your affiliations. This means that you should use your real identity in your professional accounts and save the nicknames and aliases for your personal accounts.

3. Use direct language in your writing and documentation in digital media through avoiding use of passive voice or tentative language. A good way to practice this type of language is through your emails. Instead of using tentative language like "I thought it might be a good idea to start a program on child nutrition," use direct language such as "I conducted a needs assessment in my community and found that parent education about child nutrition was lacking. As a result, I used 20% of my internship hours to build a community-based program entitled *Real Food for Real Kids.*"

4. Give due credit for the contributions of others toward your work. Similar to citing your reference materials in academic papers, it is important to post references to any copyrighted materials on your professional social media accounts. Another way to give credit is to acknowledge other agencies, stakeholders, and contributors toward projects and programs that you use as documentation of your experiences.

5. Self-edit the content you post. This translates to making sure that all the materials you post are accurate and edited for grammar and spelling. If you do make a mistake, refer back to #2 - transparency. Correct the mistake as soon as you notice it and make sure that you acknowledge the mistake by apologizing, if needed.

6. Be responsible in your posting. Make sure that you aren't negative or unprofessional on your professional sites. If you list your place of work on your personal sites, be aware that you should regard any posts as you would if they were in your professional network. By using the name of the company for which you work, you could be seen as representing their views or opinions.

7. It goes without saying that you should be professional in any written, in-person, or virtual interactions you have with others in reference to your work life. Specifically, you should not post content about controversial, potentially inflammatory topics, or non-work related topics in general. Another important aspect about professionalism in your digital identity is refraining from engaging inonline arguments or hostile communications. For example, some of you might remember the restaurateur couple who used social media to engage in personal attacks of reviewers on Yelp, leading to ongoing hostile arguments via many forms of social media (Honorof 2013).

In addition, you should avoid using slang, colloquialisms, emoticons, abbreviations, and other more casual ways of communicating in your digital representation of yourself. You should make sure any pictures related to your professional digital identity are appropriate, relevant, and work to

advance your efforts in demonstrating your trustworthiness and your sense of responsibility.

8. Be aware of privacy issues in the presentation of your work, knowledge, and experiences that become a part of your digital identity. Students in Family Science should be aware of information about individuals and families with whom they work. Permission should be obtained, and noted, for any pictures that show participants or community members in your professional digital identity.

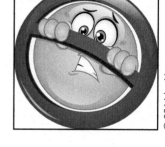

9. Related to the point above, you should make it a point to know the rules regarding publicizing information or images of your work or of people with whom you work and make sure that you follow them. Those viewing your professional digital identity will know the rules, and expect you to follow them; therefore ignorance of the rules will make it seem like you have a disregard for them—which is exactly the opposite of the impression that you would like to make.

YOUR DIGITAL IDENTITY

If you want to know more about someone you've just met, you just Google them. It's become so commonplace that Google and Facebook have become verbs! What would potential internships or employers would find out about you?

Google (or Bing or whatever) yourself using at least five additional keywords.
KEYWORDS (suggestions major, job title, university, professional keywords):
1.
2.
3.
4.
5.

What are the top 10 sites returned by the search engine? Are they personal sites or student accounts?

Results	Personal or Professional
1.	
2.	
3.	
4.	
5.	
6.	
7.	
8.	
9.	
10.	

Now, imagine that you are in the position to hire someone for an internship or entry-level position in your field. For an even more realistic experience, select a particular agency with which you'd like to work.

Search for employees of that agency, again using at least five keywords related to your professional field.

KEYWORDS:

1.

2.

3.

4.

5.

What type of results for these professionals do you see? Does their professional work or their personal sites top the search results? If you only find personal sites and no professional ones, you might want to think twice about the professionalism of the organization where you'd like to intern!

Results	Personal or Professional
1.	
2.	
3.	
4.	
5.	
6.	
7.	
8.	
9.	
10.	

Have a professor, a coworker, or a supervisor at work *that doesn't know you very well* review your Facebook, Instagram, Pinterest, Snapchat, Twitter, and whatever other social media sites you frequent. Ask them the following questions.

What types of assumptions would you make about the person in the profiles?
What type of image of the person comes to mind?
Would they hire the person in the profiles/sites?
How would they describe the person in their own words?

After completing all of these, ask yourself the question:

Would you hire your digital self?
What evidence is found in your digital identity that you would make a good intern/employee?

REFERENCES

Burrus, D. (2011). Create Social Media Guidelines to Reach Your Customer. Home Business Magazine: The Home-Based Entrepreur's Magazine, 18(1), 32–35.

Finn, G., Garner, J., & Sawdon, M. (2010). 'You're judged all the time?' Students' views on professionalism: a multicenter study. *Medical Education, 44,* 814–825.

Garner, J. & O'Sullivan, H. (2010). Facebook and the professional Behaviours of undergraduate medical students. *The Clinical Teacher, 7,* 112–115.

Gross, G. (May 29, 2012). Gartner sees huge rise in corporate social media monitoring. *Computer World.* 5/29/2012 Retrieved from http://www.computerworld.com/s/article/9227556/Gartner_sees_huge_rise_in_corporate_social_media_monitoring

Honorof, M. (May 16, 2013) How Amy's Baking Company ruined itself on social media. Tech News Daily. Retrieved from http://www.technewsdaily.com/18091-social-media-amys-baking.html

Lave, J & Wenger, E (1991). *Situated Learning: Legitimate Peripheral Participation.* New York; Cambridge University Press.

Love, D. (May 11, 2011). 17 People who were fired for using Facebook. The Business Insider. Retrieved from http://www.businessinsider.com/facebook-fired-2011-5?op=1

Mostaghhimi, A. & Crotty, B.H. (2011). Professionalism in the Digital Age. *Annals of Internal Medicine, 154(8),* 560–563.

Popkin, H. (March 27, 2009). Getting the Skinny on Twitter's Cisco Fatty. Updated on 3/27/2009. Retrieved from http://www.nbcnews.com/id/29901380/ns/technology_and_science-tech_and_gadgets/t/getting-skinny-twitters-cisco-fatty/#.U0WOPK1dU6I

PRNewswire (April 18, 2012). Thirty-Seven percent of companies use social networks to research potential job candidates, according to new CareerBuilder Survey. Retrieved from http://www.prnewswire.com/news-releases/thirty-seven-percent-of-companies-use-social-networks-to-research-potential-job-candidates-according-to-new-careerbuilder-survey-147885445.html

Who Are You on Paper?

OBJECTIVES:

➤ Generate professional self-presentation in writing
  - Email
  - Cover Letters, Resume, Thank You
➤ Generate professional writing for graduate school applications
  - Personal Statement/Statement of Goals
  - Letters of Interest/Intent
➤ Request a recommendation
  - For Graduate study
  - For employment

MAKING THE MOST OF A FIRST IMPRESSION

"Omg you're here! Ahh i need to get my s--t together now lol. Jk. Give me a ring when u can/want, my cell is [redacted]. I have class until 1230 but then im free! i will let the teacher she u will be there, shes a darling. Perhaps ill come to the end of the talk and meet you there after. Between the faculty lunch and your talk, we can chat! ill take make sure the rooms are all ready for u. See ya!" *(Wade, 2014, paragraph 2)*

What is your impression of the person who wrote the email above? What picture or ideas about this person arise for you in terms of: sex, race, age, education background, socioeconomic status, or status within the organization, etc.?

We all know the email above isn't a great example of appropriate professional correspondence. Yet we receive emails like it frequently, almost daily, and can commiserate with the person who received the one above. In fact, this was an email sent by an Ivy League university student to a prominent guest lecturer when she was acting as the liaison for the visiting professor. Surprised? So was the visiting professor. The professor was shocked to receive such an inappropriately familiar email from a student at a prestigious university, that she asked fellow well-respected faculty members ...pile a list of their *least* favorite student behaviors. The full list of professors' least favorite ...iors is included in the list of *10 Things Every College Professor Hates*—and we recommend you ...tention to avoiding these behaviors! We strongly encourage you to read the full article to un- ...and how faculty members interpret your behaviors because how you *intend* the behavior isn't ...portant as how it is interpreted.

COMMUNICATING WHO YOU ARE IN WRITING

Your writing is the first opportunity for self-presentation when interacting with potential internship sites, either through an email requesting an interview or via your cover letter and resume. Unfortunately, writing is another area where students often struggle, both with content and with professionalism.

According to our observations, students encounter difficulties when writing professionally. Students are so concerned with **not** sounding like students that their writing 'voice' sounds nothing like how they would normally speak. While there should be a higher degree of professionalism in writing versus speaking, the difference should be minimal and the writing should retain elements of the students' personalities. To summarize, don't try to be someone you aren't.

When students try to be someone else in their writing, they are unnecessarily complex and unclear. Good writing attracts readers. In other words, writing should be easy to read and follow commonsense rules (Bailey, 2010). Think about a time when you had to read and re-read a sentence over and over in order to understand what it was saying. The lack of clarity could be due to the complexity of the material, but often it is poor writing skills that leave the reader grasping to understand the main point.

Bailey (2010) recommends using Plain English, a form of written communication that is not overly formal (stilted and bureaucratic) but not text-speak or slang. Plain English uses ordinary, spoken language so sentences are easier to read, and requires that you are clear about your main point in the first couple of sentences of the document. When the main point of your document is front and center, your readers don't have to search for your intended message, directive you're giving, or the key pieces of information. Achieve clarity through using a good layout that allows the reader to easily follow the flow of information. Good physical layout requires the use of headings and/or bullets so that the essential elements stand out.

This chapter focuses on the ways students can be more professional in their written communication for your internship and for seeking employment (e.g. email, resumes, and cover letters). For students planning to apply to graduate school during or after their internships, this chapter will provide some guidance in terms of writing letters of interest and personal or goals statements for graduate applications.

10 Things Every College Professor Hates
1. Unprofessional correspondence
2. Asking "Did I miss anything important?"
3. Packing up as the class is ending
4. Asking about assignments described in the syllabus
5. Getting mad when you receive critical feedback
6. Grade grubbing
7. Messing with paper formatting
8. Padding your introductions and conclusions
9. Misinterpreting opinions as fact
10. Being too cool for school

(Adapted from Wade, 2014)

Email

Digital natives have been socialized into writing through their prolific use of text-based communication via social media and other technologies. While this brings some advantages, the disadvantages far outweigh them in a professional environment. For example, students are more likely to use slang, text-speak, or omit basic social conventions that potential employers and supervisors find necessary. The introduction to this chapter makes a strong case for this. In addition, contemporary work environments are much more likely to use email as their primary means of written communication, adding even more evidence that students should evaluate their self-presentation in email specifically. In order to help students understand self-presentation in email, this chapter looks at email professionalism from two aspects—email construction and clarity.

Since email has no visible social skills to assess, email construction influences the impression made on the receiver. For example, as you open the new email, **STOP!**—don't enter the recipient's address until *after* you've written and edited the email. By waiting to enter the recipient's address, you eliminate the possibility of sending the email before you have had the opportunity to revise, edit, and review its content. When you finally enter an email address, look at it closely to ensure that you've entered it correctly so that your recipient actually receives it. We realize this sounds extremely basic but cyberspace is full of emails that never reached their destination. Lastly, when constructing your professional emails, create a succinct yet informative subject line (Bailey, 2010). Professionals who receive upwards of 200 emails per day need to be able to easily identify the content of your email so they can prioritize tasks.

The second aspect of email professionalism is clarity. Again, Bailey (2010) provides a number of suggestions for reviewing your emails. For example, if you could only write one sentence, what would it say?

As with any good written self-presentation, make judicious use of bullets in your emails as well. Email is designed to be a briefer and more direct form of communication than other writing, and therefore your emails should be detailed yet concise. This is a difficult skill to master, so take every opportunity to refine your ability to give enough information without losing your reader. Similarly, number your paragraphs for related issues (Bailey, 2010). For unrelated points, send separate emails so that each thread contains information specific to one topic. This prevents vital information from getting lost in another topic.

As we said, email is intended to be a brief form of communication and has replaced the office memo. Therefore, send longer items using attached files rather than incorporating the information into the body of the email. Like using separate emails for unrelated points, this ensures that your recipient receives all of the information in a form that is more useful. If there are lengthy documents or those that need to be updated frequently, use an office network (if available), a shared Dropbox folder, or GoogleDocs to make sure that everyone has the most up-to-date version of the information.

How are nonverbal aspects conveyed via email? What strategies do we use in email, texts, or messaging apps to simulate these nonverbal messages? Despite their appeal and your familiarity with them, **do not** try to relay emotion using emoticons or emojis. These are acceptable in your personal communications and perhaps, in several years, will be acceptable in your informal communications with peers in the workplace. However, as a student or intern, you have not built sufficient social capital to be able to use these. Even if others in your internship site are using them, resist the temptation to include these in your emails. Why is it not ok for you but ok for others? Glad you asked; this is because you are the intern who is being constantly evaluated. Your supervisors, your colleagues, and your consumers, if you interact with the public, are evaluating everything you do and don't do whether you are earning a Pass/Fail or a letter grade, are an intern, or a new employee on a probationary period. An intern or a new employee should aim to use a level of professionalism that is just a hair above that of the others in the office.

Another good way to start evaluating your level of professional presentation in email is by doing some basic reviewing and editing. For example, do you have a salutation, a name (Ms. X, Janelle, etc), or nothing at all? Does your salutation include the correct title (Mr., Ms., or Dr.)? Is there an appropriate closing? For example, your professional emails shouldn't be signed with "Love, X". Rather, professional sign-offs such as "Best regards, Regards, Thank you," or in more formal emails, "Sincerely," are considered appropriate.

One of our pet peeves is to receive emails from students with obvious spelling and grammar mistakes in them because we know that most programs, applications, and email formats have editing built into them. We understand that sometimes students are using their phones to respond to an email, and therefore it is harder to edit due to physical limitations or screen glare. However, if you are sending an email

don't have basic spelling mistakes. For example, while writing this chapter, we received an email from a colleague saying that her *name* was

Be proper

Be sure

(Adapted from Joseph, 2014)

misspelled in an email from a new employee. The mistake was made because spell-check doesn't catch misspellings that are actual words. A common misspelling that isn't picked up is substituting 'form' for 'from.' This type of mistake is easy to overlook because your brain reads the word as 'from'; however, making a mistake in the name of a presenter is unacceptable and you should read your content very carefully before sending your email.

Lastly, while you might consider your emails private, they are actually a public document. Emails are a digital record of your communications and depending on your internship site, might be subject to oversight by your employer/internship. As the executives at SONY discovered (Paglieri, 2014), work-related emails are just as vulnerable as any other digital information and can lead to disastrous consequences if one is careless.

Cover Letters, Resumes, and Thank Yous

Either during your internship or shortly thereafter, you are probably going to start looking for a job. Of course, if you apply the content in Chapter 8, you are using your internship as a networking opportunity to help you find a job after graduation. In any event, you will still need to submit application materials like a cover letter, a resume, and, of course, follow up with a Thank You note for any interviews. This section provides an overview of how you should approach these types of professional writing and provides you with templates to use when creating your own documents.

Cover Letters. Even though many cover letters or letters of introduction are likely to be virtual rather than paper-based now, the same rules for writing an effective and impactful cover letter apply. So, regardless of the method of delivery, your cover letter is often the first opportunity you have to impress a potential internship supervisor, employer, or graduate program.

An effective cover letter provides enough information about who you are to generate interest in learning more about you while also highlighting key information in your resume that provides more detail or context than you have in your resume. Keep in mind the information earlier about maintaining your voice because it is easy to start to sound stilted when trying to craft prose detailing how awesome you are. In part, because most of us are trained to think bragging and highlighting our accomplishments is arrogant. Though you don't want to sound cocky, confidence is the goal of your cover letter. If your letter doesn't convey that you are confident in your ability to do the job/be successful in the program, why should they interview you?

We have learned that providing examples of cover letters or any other kind of writing serves to actually restrict students' writing, creating cookie cutter documents with no personality that don't really impress. Also, because family science is such a broad field **and** you should tailor your cover letter to each and every internship/job/graduate program, we've provided a different kind of template showing you what kind of information should be in each section in the Cover Letter Template at the end of this chapter. Cover letters require multiple drafts to get *just right,* so write and re-write before showing your letter to a mentor or professor to get feedback. Then re-write it a few more times.

Resumes. Most colleges and universities have career services available to students to assist with resume writing. And it's easy to find examples of resumes online so we don't spend a great deal of time outlining the sections of a resume. Rather, we think it's important for students and interns to know how to best represent their experiences and highlight their abilities—particularly when they haven't had career relevant work experiences prior to their internships.

There are two types of resumes—chronological and functional. Chronological resumes detail your work experiences, relevant non-work experiences, and coursework in a chronological format, generally working backwards. These types of resumes are more traditional and might serve you well in more formal work environments. However, chronological resumes don't necessarily represent you in the best light if the majority of your work experiences have not been related to your career goals.

That said, putting work experiences that aren't related to your major or career goals can indicate that you have initiative, know how to manage your time, or just understand how to be an employee. In many environments, employers would much rather hire someone who worked part-time to fund their own college education because that student knows how to prioritize, set goals, set boundaries, and maintain standards in two disparate environments (school vs. workplace). This often speaks to the work ethic and personal characteristics that wouldn't otherwise show up on a resume. So, while being waitstaff, a barista, or bartending during college doesn't necessarily speak to your career goals, you demonstrated a number of skills in those roles that internships and employers should be aware of.

One way to bridge the difference is to provide details about non-relevant work experiences in your cover letter to supplement the information on your resume. Mention in your cover letter how you learned to balance the coursework, leadership positions, or volunteer experiences listed on your resume with part-time work experiences. Adding this connection in your cover letter demonstrates to internships/employers/graduate programs that you understand what is required in a workplace **and** are able to be simultaneously successful in your coursework.

Functional resumes, on the other hand, might be more relevant to students who have little paid work experiences leading into their internship because their purpose is to highlight skills rather than experiences and titles. The functional resume allows students without paid work experiences to emphasize the skills they exhibited in non-paid work such as volunteerism or through community engagement to impress internship supervisors, employers, and graduate programs with capabilities.

Both of these formats have their merits and their drawbacks. Decide which format best highlights your skills and experiences or, better yet, create both! By doing so, you will be prepared for opportunities that would require either. Do your homework and pay attention to what the culture of the organization is looking for. Some organizations specify that they want a one-page resume—the old standard. A functional resume is easier to do in one page since it is about highlighting skills that you can explain in your cover letter. However, other environments are less strict about the one page limit and you might be better served to do a more comprehensive chronological resume, especially if you have had some unique experiences and opportunities that will allow you to stand out.

The bottom line is that your resume should be your personal highlight reel—expressly promoting the skills, experiences, honors, and qualities that will allow you to be notable, leaving the reader wanting to hear more.

Thank You Letters. We hope that you have written a few Thank You notes in the past, however these notes serve a different purpose than the ones you write to family for gifts. A professional Thank You note achieves a precarious balance between being professional and personal. By the time you write the Thank You, you will have met the person you are receiving it but you are still being evaluated for a position (internship/graduate school/employment).

First, your Thank You should be well-timed. Generally speaking, send a Thank You so it will be received one to three days after your interview or contact with the person. Email is a perfectly acceptable way to express your gratitude and appreciation for someone's time and attention. Sending an email the day following your contact with the person is easy and accessible. However, hand written Thank You notes are both well-received and appreciated. We certainly appreciate it when students take the time to hand write a Thank You for letters of recommendation on attractive note cards or personalized stationary. Even though email is acceptable, hand-written notes convey conscientiousness, attention to detail, and a level of personal contact that trumps an email any day. Also, sending a hand written note on personalized note cards or stationary allows you to put your name in front of them at a point when they are likely encountering *other* names and faces, so the note gives them a reminder of what they liked about you. Therefore, if you are sending a hand-written note via snail mail, make sure you time it so it is received within 3 days of your contact with the person—which sometimes means mailing it the same day as your contact.

Second, make sure that your Thank You is not generic. You know, the "Thank you for your time and the opportunity. I appreciate it." Not only does that type of note **not** allow you to shine, it actually works against you by demonstrating that once you got what you wanted (the interview) you aren't going to take any extra effort. When you look at the Thank You Template at the end of this chapter, pay attention to making sure that you add something personal in your note—not about *you* though. For example, if you discovered that you shared a common interest or place with the interviewer, take the time to mention it.

It was great to talk to a fellow Atlanta Braves fan. I can't wait to see IMPORTANT PERSON play this year.

A better way to make a connection related to the program or internship is to mention something that you learned about them or their organization.

I was fascinated to learn that your newest community stakeholder is PROJECT X. I have been admiring their work with POPULATION, since I've volunteered with COMMUNITY AGENCY over the past two years. PROJECT X sounds like they serve a similar population.

See what we did there? Even your Thank You is a tool for subtle self-promotion. By connecting something you learned about the graduate program or organization to your experiences or skills, you continue to highlight the ways you would be a great fit for them—and ultimately, why they should select you!

STANDING OUT FROM THE COMPETITION FOR GRADUATE PROGRAMS

We read though students' graduate applications regularly and find that students often lose their voice when trying to sound like they'd be a good fit for the graduate program. Students try to write about the things they think graduate admissions want to hear in the way they think they should sound as a graduate student. But, when you do that, you end up sounding like every other applicant who is doing exactly the same thing. When you are preparing your written materials for graduate school applications, reread it through the eyes of an administrator. Evaluate whether or not the document really represents **you** as well as if your document helps you stand out from your competition.

Personal Statement/Statement of Goals

In addition to written self-presentation in your cover letters and resumes, graduate programs often want you to submit writing samples in the form of personal statements or statements of goals. These types of documents are dual purposed for graduate programs: they allow graduate programs to get a sense of who you are or how well their program fits with your goals **and** they provide examples of your writing abilities.

In the same vein as the other written forms of self-presentation, your personal statements and statements of goals for graduate programs should strike the balance between professionalism and demonstrating your voice. The first part is often easier than the second since you can ask professors, instructors, and other persons in your desired field to review the content of your statement.

Each university or graduate program has their own set of questions that they would like applicants to answer, so we can't provide you with a step-by-step guide to answering them. However, we can provide a common set of questions that programs *might* want you to reflect upon (See Table 3.1. Graduate School Statements) as well as come general guidelines for ways to stand out.

One of the most common mistakes we see in students personal statements are not being specific enough and over-use of jargon. Students tend to think that throwing in a bunch of words that are common to the field is better because the language sounds smart and demonstrates some familiarity with the field. Sort of true—when students *over*-use jargon it is like they are trying too hard, desperately clinging to vocabulary to make the point that they belong in graduate school. Judicious use of meaningful vocabulary (notice we didn't say jargon) demonstrates that you have already become familiar with the lexicon of your field and have started to become socialized into the discipline. Unfortunately, overuse of jargon means that you can't explain what you know in commonly used language and indicates that you might not actually know what you are saying.

TABLE 3.1. Common Questions for Graduate School Statements.

How do your personal experiences inform your career goals?
How did your personal experiences/background influence your choice of graduate study
How do your academic experiences inform or influenced your goals/choice of graduate study/ thinking?
Explain how this program/field will assist you in your short and long term goals?
Explain your long term career goals and how this degree will assist you in those goals?
Why did you select this particular program/institution/field of study?
How will this program prepare you to work with the populations you plan to work with?
Which faculty members in the program would you like to work with?
Please explain how your career goals or areas of interest align with current faculty members' interests?

Students are also often guilty of being too vague in their writing and simplifying what are often complex topics. For example, compare the two sentences below and determine which one you think would make the most impact on a prospective graduate program.

"I have known that I wanted to work with children since I volunteered at my church day care center. I have such a heart for children and how they can be so different from one another at the same age."

"I first learned how exciting working with young children could be when I began volunteering in my church day care center. I was fascinated by the way children who were the same age could vary based on their different developmental trajectories. That experience launched my interest in working with young children in ways that provide developmentally appropriate support and I have been fortunate enough to find volunteer and internships opportunities that allowed me to continue to learn about the complexity and diversity of young children."

The examples above contain the same content—but one pays more attention to detail, provides better insight into the knowledge and motivation of the writer, and contains more information about who they are as a person. Often students forget that they know what they intend to say or what they mean, so they leave out critical details that add depth to their writing, a big mistake when your audience is a group of graduate administrators have to weed through hundreds of documents in order to select the best candidates. Your best strategy is to be specific without crossing the line into minutia.

Personal statements for graduate school aren't a last-minute endeavor. In fact, there should be multiple drafts before you approach professors, instructors, or supervisors for their opinions. Each time you review your personal statement, consider:

- Are you being concise and specific, or verbose and vague?
- Does your voice shine through?
- Does your statement reflect your interests, goals, and plans?
- Do you mention relevant experiences (academic and personal)?
- Do you connect your career goals with the interests of current faculty?
- Is it clear how you will reflect positively on the program if they accept you?

ASKING FOR RECOMMENDATIONS

Though not specific to how you represent yourself in writing, many students are unsure how to ask for recommendations or what type of information they should provide to ensure that they receive good recommendations. The best rule to remember is to provide everything the recommender needs. If the recommender has to work to find information about you, your chosen programs, or the recommendation process, it will take away from their ability to spend time writing you a glowing recommendation (See *Information You Should Provide to Recommenders*).

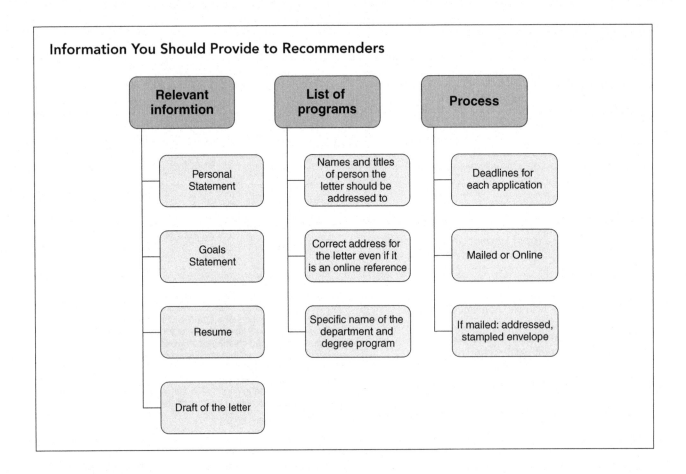

Carefully consider which people should provide you with your letters of recommendation. First, who can provide you with a **good** recommendation? Just because you got an A in a course and it's relevant, doesn't mean the person can or will write you a positive recommendation. For example, if you were habitually late, often absent, or frequently checking your social media accounts during class, you probably shouldn't ask that person for a recommendation (trust us—we notice those things!). Select faculty members that know your name, know you by sight, and whom you have had interactions with *outside of class*. Think of it this way, you always attend class, are an active contributor during class, have done well with your coursework, and the class is relevant to your career goals—if the faculty member doesn't know **you** outside of what you've contributed to class, she will probably only write about those things. The vast majority of recommendations say positive things, so if the only positive things your letters say is that you went to class and you contributed…your application will fade into the background. Getting to know faculty by visiting their office and having a conversation about the class, your interests, or anything will help that faculty member feel more connected to you and will enable her to add more personal comments in your letter allowing you to shine.

This seems fairly obvious, but we think its important to mention that you should start developing these relationships with faculty **before** you are in need of a recommendation. For example, volunteer (notice I said volunteer) to help them with a research project that aligns with your interests; do an independent study about a topic related to their class but allows you to read more in depth on the topic or meet with the faculty member regularly; or find reasons to pop into their office to say hello. By making the effort to get to know faculty members throughout your academic career, they will have far more information that they can share in their enthusiastic recommendation letters.

APPLYING YOUR KNOWLEDGE

Using the information presented in this chapter and the rating system provided in the Professional Writing Assessment, evaluate the sample text at the beginning of this chapter.

List at least five of the mistakes the writer of the email made:

1.

2.

3.

4.

5.

List at least three other mistakes made in the sample text that weren't included in the assessment?

1.

2.

3.

Using the same information and Professional Writing Assessment, evaluate your own professional writing skills by assessing a recent email you've sent to a professor, supervisor, or employer.

List at least three of the mistakes you made:

1.

2.

3.

List five ways you could improve your writing skills before going on your internship?

1.

2.

3.

4.

5.

What are at least three strategies you could use to help yourself build these skills?

1.

2.

3.

PROFESSIONAL WRITING SKILLS ASSESSMENT

		Yes	No	N/A
1.	Uses tentative language (see chapter for examples)			
2.	Uses the same phrases or clauses two or more times per paragraph (ex: with regard to, for example, and so forth, however, therefore, etc.)			
3.	Uses the same phrases or clauses two or more times per paragraph in two or more paragraphs			
4.	Uses jargon			
5.	Uses headings			
6.	Uses bullets to summarize lengthy information			
7.	There are numbered paragraphs for related issues			
8.	Uses text-speak			
9.	Uses abbreviations (exceptions include universally accepted abbreviations such as states)			
10.	Uses slang			
11.	Reads the way you speak (generally)			
12.	The main point of the document is in the first 1-2 sentences			
13.	There are spelling errors			
14.	There are grammatical errors			
15.	There is a closing statement			
16.	Uses informative subject line			
17.	Uses an attachment for a longer document			
18.	Uses emoticons, emojis, or other icon based symbols			
19.	There is a salutation			
20.	There is an appropriate signature			

Scoring

Add up the total number of 'N/A' responses and subtract from 20. This will be your denominator.

Give yourself 1 point for each 'yes' on numbers 5–7, 11, 12, 15–17, and 19–20. Add one point for each 'no' on numbers 1–4, 8–10, 13–14, and 18. Divide this number by your denominator. Multiply the result by 100. Find your percentage below to evaluate the professionalism of your writing.

50% or below: You have some serious work to do in order to bring your professional writing skills up to an appropriate level to even consider an internship experience. During internship experiences, students are required to interact with potential future colleagues, network with potential employers, and interact with the community. In order to represent yourself, your department and your college or university well, you should work with resources to improve your professional writing before engaging in your internship. Use the resources at your institution to improve your ability to communicate in writing. For example, writing centers, career services offices, student tutors, and others can provide resources, review your writing, and create a strategy with you. Another option is to use this assessment to create a list of do's and don'ts to review your own writing.

50-80%: Though you have some of the basics down, your professional writing still needs some work. Pay attention to the items on the assessment that could improve both the interpretation of the content as well as the impression your writing makes on the recipient. Create a list of your particular foibles and develop a reminder system for yourself, focusing on the positive attributes of your writing while correcting the less impressive ones.

80-99%: You are doing most of the things you should and few of the things you shouldn't in your professional writing. Review the items on the list to find ways to improve your professional writing. For example, students often fall into the habit of omitting a salutation and a closing because they are so used to texting where these conventions are unnecessary. Pay attention to the ways your writing can improve the impression you make on potential employers through your internship.

100%: Great job! You are doing all of the things you should and none of the things you shouldn't based on this list. Even though you've got this down, you should still make sure you edit each and every professional communication to make sure none of those mistakes slip through!

Cover Letter Sample

Date

You MUST put an actual person's name here. Use your technological savvy to find out who this should be addressed to - even if it means you go 'old school' by calling to find out!

NAME
Title/Role in the organization
Address
City, State Zip

Using the correct title shows that you've done your homework and are being respectful of their senior position - one you hope they will use to hire you!

Also, need an actual name. DO NOT put "To Whom it May Concern" or "Dear Admissions"

Salutation,

Also make sure you use the correct title (Mr., Mrs., Dr., Reverend) AND use the correct pronouns in the body of your letter.

Your first paragraph should express your interest in the position or program – noting the specific name of the position, listing number if applicable, and how you learned about the position. If you know someone who works for the company, this is where you would mention the person – but make sure you ask permission from them first. Also, make sure you are enthusiastic in this paragraph but not unprofessional.

This next paragraph should begin to outline your qualifications for the position by mentioning what is in your resume but also providing more details about why that job/skill/experience prepares you for or makes you the best candidate for the position/graduate program. You can use more than one paragraph for this portion if needed to separate your experiences into relevant categories (e.g. volunteer experiences, research, jobs, or the ways different experiences have shaped specific skills).

You absolutely, positively need to tailor this to each and every position you apply for. Sending a generic letter is a surefire way to not get an interview.

(For Graduate applications) This paragraph should tell graduate administrators what your professional goals are: what are your plans for your career? What is your area of interest in research or clinical populations that you'd like to work with? How will you use your degree in a way that will reflect positively on the program and the field?

This last paragraph should be your big finish! Summarize why they should hire you/admit you without repeating what you've said before. Leave them impressed and wanting to know more, but with enough information to decide to interview you.
Respectfully Submitted/Best Regards,

Your signature

Your name

Your title or special designations (if appropriate)

Your title might be from your internship or special designations might be Certified Family Life Educator (CFLE) or other piece of information that will help you stand out.

Date

Salutation,

You should use an appropriate salutation. Even if you were asked to call the person by their first name, err on the side of formality when sending the Thank You note (e.g. Dr. Mrs. etc)

Your first paragraph should express your appreciation for their time and the opportunity to learn more about them.

This next paragraph should add specific details from your conversation, interview, or what you learned about the organization during your interaction with them. Adding these details reminds them of the connection they made with you shows your attention to detail, and your enthusiasm for their organization.

Thank them again in your final paragraph, offer to provide any further information they might need, and finally state that you look forward to hearing from them or express confidence in your fit with the organization.

Best Regards,

Your name

Developing Your Goals

OBJECTIVES

By the end of this chapter you should be able to:

➤ Define different types of goals
➤ Identify personal, professional and civic goals
➤ Understand how to advocate for yourself using goals
➤ Conduct a personal needs/goals assessment

The goal of internships is to provide you with the opportunity to apply your academic knowledge in the real world. An **internship** is a field-based learning experience that allows you to spend **quality** time reflecting critically on the knowledge you have learned, as well as who you are and who you want to become professionally. During this time, you apply your knowledge of the social sciences through observation and practice. In an internship, you use the theoretical frameworks as you practice in the field—**praxis.**

During your internship, you will be expected to develop an understanding of the respective mission, policies, and services of the agency sponsoring your experience. You are expected to develop professional skills and work habits that will allow you to transition into your chosen career. It is important to recognize that the internship is not just about launching you into a career, although that can be a positive outcome. Completing an internship in the human services field allows you to explore yourself, while learning about the inner workings of an agency or organization, and helps you understand the contextual influences that impact yours and others' lives on a regular basis (Parilla & Hesser, 1998). Whether you are awarded academic credit for an internship or not, the first priority in developing, reflecting, and evaluating your goals and objectives is to reflect critically on your past, present and future experiences (Parilla & Hesser, 1998). Without this step, you are not learning about yourself or mastering the concepts learned in your department/college (Parilla & Hesser, 1998).

To take full advantage of the opportunity to complete an internship, we recommend conceptualizing the experience using Kolb's Experiential Learning Theory (Kolb, Boyatzis & Mainemelis, 2001). This theory suggests that you will have concrete experiences as well as abstract conceptualizations. You will begin the internship with concrete experiences; you will make observations about these, and then eventually reflect upon what has happened. As you go through this process multiple times, you combine your reflections and mentally develop abstract conceptualizations of your experience (Kolb, Boyatzis & Mainemelis, 2001). Much like young children accommodate and assimilate their experiences to learn, so do you using this process. To begin understanding what these concrete experiences and abstract conceptualizations might actually look like, we will discuss goal development as a framework for your experience.

TYPES OF GOALS

Knowledge

During an internship, students can acquire new knowledge (Parilla & Hesser, 1998). Although the information gained will be unique to each student and each placement, some examples may include learning how an agency operates, how to write a grant, how to effectively engage children of varying abilities, or perhaps learning how to operate within a professional environment. Regardless of what new knowledge you acquire during your internship, it is important that you make a conscious effort to open yourself up to new experiences and new information. In the face of experiences that may challenge you, trust the process and the professionals around you to provide the safe and supportive environment you need to succeed.

You may find that you acquire new knowledge naturally as you attend your internship each day, but you may also discover a new passion or interest that inspires you to learn more (Parilla & Hesser, 1998). As we will discuss in the last chapter, developing a project during your internship can enable you to explore a topic of interest in more depth, hopefully creating a product that not only meets your needs to learn more, but your agency's needs to meet its mission.

Another way to learn during your internship is to make connections between your academic knowledge and your internship experience (Parilla & Hesser, 1998). In our program, students must obtain an internship that enables them to apply our departmental objectives. Broadly, those include integrating and applying theory, learning about research and ethical practices, demonstrating and disseminating knowledge of physical, cognitive and social emotional development of individuals and families, as well as the ability to critically evaluate the interdependent systems in which individuals and families live. As you can see, it is quite important that our students have the opportunity to continue learning these key concepts through practice in an internship. Philosophically, we believe that it is imperative that all students use their educational knowledge to become competent and confident professionals in human services fields.

Whether you are acquiring or applying knowledge, keep in mind what the main goal of any internship is: putting theory into practice. As you learn and think more about what your goals are in an internship, remember to keep this bigger picture at the forefront of your experience. Once you begin the internship, it is easy to get bogged down in discovering the day-to-day operations, or worrying about how your supervisor and colleagues perceive you. Although you may be treated as a colleague (employee), you are a student whose primary goal is to have an educational experience and learn. Advocate for yourself as a learner and avoid the mentality that you are supposed to know how to "do things" as an employee without support or guidance (Parilla & Hesser, 1998). You deserve an experience that allows you to grow personally, professionally and civically, so be mindful of your goals and communicate those clearly to your university and site supervisor. We cannot read minds, and if we are to advocate for your experience, we need to be informed. Additionally, your university supervisor may act as a mediator between you and your supervisor, not in the face of challenge (although that may occur), but to reiterate both departmental/college and your goals clearly (Parilla & Hesser, 1998). When students call or contact us with concerns in their placement, our first question is always, "Have you communicated your needs to your supervisor?" In many cases, the answer is no and we can take that opportunity to help the student work through the issue at hand. At the end of the day, clear communication is key to keeping everyone on the same page with the ability to provide the educational experience that you seek.

During the process of exploring internship sites, it is important that you understand what requirements your department/college has for qualified internship sites. It is also important that you find an internship that allows you to integrate those requirements with your professional desires, and in my experience, in doing so, students have a much richer experience.

Skills

During an internship, you will most certainly gain professional skills that are necessary for future success. One of the most important skills you can learn is time management. Many of our students are enrolled in additional coursework, are employed and committed to extracurricular activities. Your internship will undoubtedly be a priority (it should be), so you must learn to navigate various roles during the internship semester. Use the tools in Chapter 1 to keep your life in order and use your supervisor and colleagues as models, as you observe their time management skills. Recall how you spent 168 hours when you conducted the exercise. Have you changed your habits to use your time more effectively? Why or why not, and what adjustments have you made?

© 2015 by Rawpixel. Used under license of Shutterstock, Inc.

You may also decide that you need to improve your communication, as most people do. Think about the last time you had a professional conversation in person or on the phone. Were you comfortable? Why or why not? Although the Millennial Generation (most likely you) has grown up with more technology than any other generation, digital natives, they are often also described as digital refugees—the notion that technology is the answer to everything, even communication (Coombes, 2009). Unfortunately, this is not necessarily the case in the professional worlds they enter. Think about your preferred method of communication; what is it? How do you feel when you must utilize a non-preferred method? To reach a diverse audience, agencies cannot solely rely on technology as you know it. Phone calls must be made, and you will have to talk to people while others are in the room. Are they listening to you and criticizing your delivery? Maybe, but maybe not. Regardless, is talking on the phone a skill you need to develop, or does it reach wider than that? Do you really need to learn how to utilize technology appropriately in a professional environment?

Attitude

During an internship, you will face challenges. These may occur within you or with others, but in any case, are often the result of attitudes. Remember when you identified your biases in Chapter 1? Which of these can you work on during your internship? When you face colleagues or clients that challenge you, how will you approach the situation? If you take advantage of the internship opportunity and use each challenge, or triumph for that matter, as a learning opportunity or moment that teaches you something, then you can ensure that you make the most out of your experience.

Attitude is everything!

© 2015 by Ivelin Radkov. Used under license of Shutterstock, Inc.

As you enter the professional world after your internship and college, you will need to know how to monitor your attitudes. It is rare, impossible even, to believe that every environment and person you interact with will agree with everything you do, so although we are not asking you to change what you believe, be open to hearing others' perspectives and learning from them. At the end of the day, if all you did is reaffirm your attitudes, then it was a valuable experience.

TYPES OF LEARNING GOALS

Because goals are individualized and placement specific, you can begin your process by asking the following questions, suggested by Parilla & Hesser (1998). "(1) what you know you know; (2) what you know that you don't know; and (3) what you don't know that you don't know" (Parilla & Hesser, 1998, p. 319). Use your academic knowledge to answer the first question, and perhaps even the second. The answer to the third question will come with time, experience and reflection.

We all know that it is easy to forget information once you put your pencil down after an exam. The goal in the internship is to reaffirm your knowledge and utilize it so that it becomes ingrained into your long-term memory.

Now that you are armed with information about the endless possibilities you have in your internship, complete the activities in this chapter. Remember that these are all fluid documents that may shift as you continue throughout the semester, or during your internship. Use these activities to advocate for your experience and develop a learning agreement between yourself, the department/college, and your internship site. In many cases, your department and the site may have their own agreement that must be completed, but attempting to define your goals and expectations for the experience multiple times only allows you to learn more about yourself in the process, ensuring that you enter the field with eyes wide open and the ability to know exactly what you need to do to make the most of your internship.

Take a moment to learn more about your departmental requirements. What set of criteria must an internship site meet to fulfill departmental guidelines? Based on the activities you have completed thus far, what do you *think* you want to learn about? How do departmental goals and your goals match?

Goals do not only address knowledge, skills and attitudes; they also address your personal, professional and civic identities. Review the activities you completed in Chapter 1 to determine how these identities translate into the professional world of internships. How do your values impact what you want in a professional environment?

© 2015 by Rasstock. Used under license of Shutterstock, Inc.

Personal

Based on your Life Map activity, what aspects of your personal identity are important to you? For example, we have had supervisors explain that they must be transparent with students about services they offer to young adults. When victims of sexual assault seek out their agency, they educate them about all of their options, including abortion. Because they understand that this is a personal and controversial topic to many, they are forthright with potential interns to ensure that the student makes the decision to pursue the opportunity knowing what they may encounter. These are situations that you may face when seeking an internship, so it is important to know what you are willing to experience, and how your personal identity and values impact the environment you seek.

You must also consider your strengths and weaknesses, as well as how much you are willing to confront your weaknesses. If you know that your learning is hindered by independence, and you prefer to work in groups, or find it difficult to take initiative, you must decide how much that will inform the internship environment. We challenge you to become comfortable with the uncomfortable and find an environment that forces, but supports, you to be more independent and self-sufficient. Recall the lists of strengths and weaknesses you made and ask yourself: "What type of environment will allow me to grow?"

Professional

Whether you are learning professional skills or knowledge for yourself, or are working with others to learn more about professional environments and relationships, you must first assess where you want to go and how you want to get there. Do you need to develop skills related to organization, communication, management, presentation/facilitation, programming, evaluation, case management, etc.? How will you do this? Ideally, you gain many professional skills during your internship, but you must understand what you need, what you want, and how these skills will benefit you in the future.

In a moment, we will discuss how to use NCFR's Family Life Education Content Areas and Competencies to develop your professional goals. In the meantime, also consider the specific professional skills you need in a chosen career track. Take this opportunity to search for professionalism in the "_____ field." Whether you select 'youth development' or 'therapy', what do the professionals in your field need to succeed?

Civic

Throughout this text, we have discussed the importance of a civic or community identity. You may initially think about your civic goals related to a place-based community that you want to learn more about, or potentially put down roots in. Perhaps you want to explore a certain city, neighborhood, or community of people. If this is the case, then include these in your goals. Because this process is individualized, a goal of learning more about working with young children with autism in a rural community is relevant to your experience.

As you begin to frame your internship experience with goals, remember to consciously connect how your goals address personal, professional, and civic identities, as well as how they relate to knowledge, skills and attitudes. You should find that your goals are interdependent, and that once you write down one, you will experience a snowball effect and that first goal will lead you to the second, which leads you to the third, and so on. It can be difficult at first to fully articulate what it is you want out of your internship, so take your time and know that you will have many opportunities to refine your ideas.

USING YOUR NETWORK

Peers

If the thought of just brainstorming ideas on your own is daunting, use your peer network. It is helpful to find other students at the same point in their internship process as you, as well as those interested in the same topic area. Use each other to critically think about what you want to learn. In many cases, you or your peers will have volunteer experiences to draw from, and you can share important historical knowledge with one another.

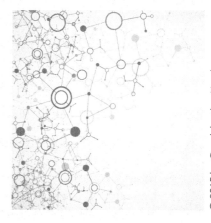

© 2015 by Omelchenko. Used under license of Shutterstock, Inc.

Potentially more helpful is contacting peers who are currently in the middle of the internship, or who have completed it. If you are interested in completing your internship in a certain location, ask your university supervisor or the placement for the contact information of current or former interns. You can bet that these students will have valuable experiences to share with you, especially regarding the types of responsibilities they have, and what they feel they have been able to learn. In our program, we invite former students back to campus to share their stories, and we have student testimonial videos on our website for current students to browse and learn from throughout their process.

Internship Supervisors

To get straight to the source, you should communicate with a potential internship supervisor. In our experience, they are people just like you, and they want you to be an intern just as much as you want to be an intern. It is easy to forget that they were once students like you, and that they actually enjoy working with students. So if you remember nothing else from this section, remember that internship supervisors want to support your learning. They are passionate about what they do and want to share that passion with you.

As you explore your interests and refine your goals, talk to them. In our department, we invite internship supervisors to campus to participate in an *Internship Fair*. Students browse the informational posters or brochures that supervisors bring, sharing their resume in the process. This allows students to not only practice professional communication, but to engage directly with the source and ask them important questions about potential responsibilities, or to learn anything at all about who they are and what they do. Each semester, supervisors and students walk away excited and invigorated by the prospect of learning.

If your department/college does not offer an opportunity like this, then make it for yourself. Contact a stakeholder at a potential site and ask them if you can meet them to learn more about what they do. Initially, you can treat this as an *Informational Interview* and gather data about their educational background, professional experiences and current responsibilities. At the end of the interview, you can inquire about potential internship opportunities and get your foot in the door.

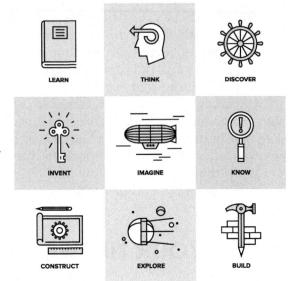

CONDUCTING RESEARCH & DEVELOPING GOALS

Once you have identified potential placements, to learn more about these options, complete the *Conducting Research activity in the Applying Your Knowledge* section of this chapter. Once you have learned more about your options, you should develop goals that address your personal, professional and civic learning objectives, that may be about knowledge, skills or attitudes. To help you complete the *Goals Activity,* refer to the list below developed by the National Council on Family Relations.

LIST OF COMPETENCIES FLE SUBSTANCE AREA

INTERPERSONAL SKILLS AND PROFESSIONAL CONDUCT
- Building rapport
- Using listening skills
- Respecting differences of opinion
- Observing confidential practices
- Following the chain of command
- Using empathy
- Communicating verbally
- Practicing cultural sensitivity
- Appreciating/honoring diversity
- Interviewing
- Engaging in a self-awareness activity
- Advocating for a group or an individual
- Attending a conference
- Setting personal/professional boundaries
- Modeling attitudes and behaviors that demonstrate ethical values

ASSESSMENT AND EVALUATION SKILLS
- Performing strength-based assessments
- Researching feasibility of programs
- Surveying participants
- Compiling quarterly reports
- Evaluating programs
- Conducting a focus group
- Grading papers
- Developing learning outcomes

- Reviewing literature
- Collecting/quantifying data
- Preparing progress reports
- Rating/testing participants

WRITING AND MATERIALS DEVELOPMENT

- Writing a memorandum
- Preparing a case study
- Developing handouts/overheads
- Creating a promotional flier
- Writing a program critique
- Assisting with/writing a grant
- Developing a website
- Completing documentation
- Writing a news release/public service message
- Corresponding with other professionals
- Designing a brochure
- Drafting policies and procedures

PLANNING AND ORGANIZATION

- Planning an event
- Updating information
- Prioritizing responsibilities
- Streamlining a process
- Developing checklists
- Serving on a committee
- Managing time
- Adhering to a budget
- Participating in strategic planning
- Scheduling activities or volunteers
- Creating forms
- Creating a promotional campaign

PROGRAM DEVELOPMENT AND INFORMATION APPLICATION

- Modifying an existing program
- Visiting model programs for ideas
- Creating a program budget
- Developing a position statement
- Creating a mission statement
- Developing goals and objectives
- Collecting information/materials
- Researching funding resources
- Adapting information into learning principles
- Establishing program and/or participant criteria
- Selecting appropriate activities
- Developing curriculum

PRESENTATION SKILLS AND TEACHING METHODS

- Facilitating an educational group
- Staffing an information booth/table
- Participating on a panel discussion
- Training/orienting volunteers
- Making a presentation
- Chairing a meeting

- Leading an activity
- Conducting a field trip
- Teaching a learning module
- Creating hands-on learning experiences
- Sharing research results with peers
- Advising program participants

Each of these competencies corresponds to the vertical axis of the CFLE Matrix, found at the end of this chapter.

Remember that your goals are fluid and will evolve over time. However, use your objectives as a way to advocate for your internship. When you discuss specific responsibilities, make sure you present information that allows your supervisor to know what you want to learn. When presented to a supervisor, it demonstrates the amount of thought you have put into your internship finding process. Remember, they want to share their passion with you, so if it is clear that you are passionate about learning; this is a positive step in the right direction for securing a placement. To take these basic ideas and refine them, complete the *Developing a Learning Plan* activity in the *Applying Your Knowledge* section of this chapter. After developing goals and specific learning methods, reflect on what types of goals you have. Are they related to personal, professional or civic growth? Are they related to knowledge or skills you want to gain, or attitudes you want to confirm or alter?

© 2015 by Trueffelpix. Used under license of Shutterstock, Inc.

Your department/college or placement might require that you complete an application. Regardless of whether or not you are required to complete a formal agreement, we also discussed developing an individual learning agreement. During the process of exploring your options, you should consider the following things. We have a *Checklist* at the end of this chapter, so you should not only answer them, but keep track of each to ensure that you have covered your bases.

Once you have an internship, prepare yourself for the experience. After securing a placement site, make arrangements to visit and shadow an intern or supervisor. In some cases, your site may be out-of-town or state. We recommend that you make arrangements to have a phone/Skype/Google Hangout meeting.

Objective: This visit should allow you to see what your internship experience will look like. It can be scary enough to begin your internship on the first day, so prepare yourself by gaining a deeper understanding of what you will do once you get there. This can be an excellent way to transition into training as you will already be familiar with the environment and the people.

1. Before the visit: Review your *Agency Research* assignment and understand the agency's mission and services; also look for a volunteer FAQ or guide sheet
2. During the visit: Ask questions!
   - Observe the individual you are shadowing and record what tasks they are doing.
   - Observe the environment: can you see yourself there?
   - Observe the 'clients.' What populations are served?
   - If you found a volunteer guide, ask what you can do that is *different*. If you did not find one, ask for information about volunteer responsibilities to determine what you can do that is *different*.
   - Ask what on-going or potential needs the agency has and whether your internship project could address them.
   - Ask a potential supervisor what their *supervision style* is, i.e. nondirective, collaborative or directive (Slick, 2000).

> If you are meeting with the supervisor directly, ask the individual or past interns. If it is a recent placement, ask for past students' contact information if you want to learn more from an *insider*. If you are unable to observe or visit your agency for confidentiality purposes, please ask a current intern, the director, or your supervisor questions about their daily tasks, environment and populations served.
> 3. After the visit: Reflect
>   • Would you change your response from the *Agency Research* assignment with regards to how this internship will contribute to your academic development?
>   • Explain how you will balance your internship responsibilities with other commitments.
>
> Write a reflective summary of your visit and complete the *Intern Shadow* form at the end of this chapter, and use it as evidence that you completed this exercise.

And finally, before you begin your internship, in addition to your learning agreement or application, we advise that you also complete an Internship Agreement, which outlines expectations from you during the experience.

The *Internship Agreement* we have provided is an example, which you may choose to use in its entirety, or adapt to fit your own needs. Many of the areas addressed are discussed in detail in remainder of this text, so you can use that information to make modifications if necessary.

CONDUCTING RESEARCH

Answer each of the questions below for **three agencies.** To make the most of this opportunity, do not copy and paste this information from their websites; interpret and write in your words to identify potential questions that need clarifications.

Before you get started, determine the *most appropriate or relevant* way to find and document this information. Some students may prefer to go directly to the organization and ask questions or volunteer, while others prefer to use the internet. Additionally, the presentation of this content can be adapted to fit your needs. For example, you may find it more helpful to have the information in a poster, video or podcast, summarized list, or a traditional paper. At the end of the day, you should use this as an opportunity to learn about an organization that will impact your future. To that end, you need to determine what that process looks like for you.

Part 1: Answer these questions broadly, not for a specific site necessarily.

1. Identify how specific departmental/college courses have prepared you to complete an internship.

2. Identify how other courses at your university have prepared you to complete an internship.

Part 2: Research three agencies to learn more about your options in order to make an educated decision about where you want to secure an internship.

1. Provide the name of the agency.

2. Describe the agency mission.

3. What services are offered? To whom?

4. Why are these services offered?

5. Who provides these services? Describe the types of staff members that work there.

6. Is the agency a business, non-profit, government body, or something else? Please explain.

7. How is the 'agency' affected by the external environment, i.e. policies, laws, etc.?

8. Is the agency, or its personnel, affiliated with a Professional Organization (i.e. NAEYC, NCFR, and AAMFT)? Explain.

9. What relationships does the 'agency' have with the community?
   a. Look at *upcoming events, news,* or *board of director members affiliations.*

   b. Some websites may include sections like *our partners.*

Part 3: Answer these questions for **each** placement to determine your best match.

   1. How will **each** internship placement contribute to your academic development?
   a. Describe your personal learning objectives, related to your discipline, as they may differ if you're exploring diverse settings.

   2. How will **each** internship placement help you obtain your career goals?

Part 4

Provide a summative statement with positives and negatives for each placement. Explain which environment you think will be best for you.

Use the CFLE Matrix and place a check mark in the box that relates to potential internship responsibilities, and that meets your goal criteria.

CFLE SUBSTANCE AREA/COMPETENCY MATRIX

	1. Families in Society	2. Internal Dynamics of Families	3. Human Growth & Development	4. Human Sexuality	5. Interpersonal Relationships	6. Family Resource Management	6. Family Resource Management	7. Parenting Education & Guidance	8. Family Law & Public Policy	9. Ethics	10. Methodology
A. Interpersonal Skills/ Professional Conduct											
B. Assessment & Evaluation Skills											
C. Writing & Materials Development											
D. Planning & Organization											
E. Program Development/ Information Application											
F. Presentation Skills/ Teaching Methods											

From *Pathways to Practice: A Family Life Education Practicum/Internship Handbook* (2002); revised 2014 and provided courtesy of Bryce Dickey, Karen Blaisure, Lori Farrer, & Kristy Smith; Western Michigan University.

Goals Activity

Use your list of three organizations from *Conducting Research* and select your FIRST choice. Select THREE substance areas (top row) that are relevant. For each substance area, select at least ONE competency (column) and write AT LEAST THREE learning objectives.

For example, an internship with the Boys and Girls Club will allow me to learn about families in society, human growth and development and interpersonal relationships.

- I will learn about *families in society* by engaging families through **material and program development** (2 competencies).
- I will learn about *human growth and development* as I work on afterschool **program development** for the children.
- I will learn about *interpersonal relationships* as I gain **professional conduct skills** with my colleagues, and as I **teach** the children in the afterschool program.

1.

2.

3.

Developing a Learning Plan

Directions: Use your Agency Research & CFLE Objective worksheet to help you identify specific learning goals you have for your internship.

Proposed Agency	

Identify 5 Goals (general) with corresponding learning methods (specific)

For example:

Goal 1:	Learn about being a program manager
Objectives:	1. Conduct informational interviews 2. Assist in writing a grant 3. Attend meetings or conference with supervisor 4. Schedule activities and/or manage volunteers
Goal 2:	Improve my professional communication skills
Objectives:	1. Read a book or articles on communication 2. Communicate with my supervisor AND others in the agency on a regular basis 3. Assist supervisor or colleague on agency report 4. Prepare for and help facilitate an agency meeting
Goal 3:	Understand the day-to-day responsibilities of being a (nurse, therapist, counselor)
Objectives:	1. Correspond with supervisor and other professionals about day-to-day "to-do's" 2. Participate in training or continuing professional education 3. Work with supervisor on patient intake forms/documentation 4. Collect information/materials that can be resources for professionals and/or patients

Additional Sample Goals:
Demonstrate mastery of program development.
Demonstrate interpersonal skills.
Demonstrate professionalism.
Demonstrate proficiency in community assessments.
Demonstrate application of knowledge in applied setting.

Goal 1:	
Objectives:	
Goal 2:	
Objectives:	
Goal 3:	
Objectives:	
Goal 4:	
Objectives:	
Goal 5:	
Objectives:	

Internship Checklist

- [ ] Is the internship paid? Is this okay in your department/college?

- [ ] Is travel required? Will you be responsible for your own expenses related to this?

- [ ] Do you need liability insurance?

- [ ] Do you need to provide a background check?

- [ ] Do you need to provide documentation of immunizations or physical?

- [ ] Do you need to provide proof of health insurance?

- [ ] Does your department/college require legal paperwork, i.e. Memorandum of Understanding/ Agreement?

- [ ] What educational background or how many years' experience does your supervisor need to have?

- [ ] How will the agency train you?

- [ ] How accessible will your internship supervisor be to you? Will you schedule weekly meetings?

- [ ] How will you remain connected to your university department/college?

Intern Shadow

Student's Name	
Contact Information	
Agency Name	
Contact's Name	
Contact's Title	
Contact's Email	
Contact's Phone Number	
Contact's Signature	
*Your signature verifies that this student visited or phoned your agency and shadowed a professional.	
Student's Signature	

Internship Agreement

It is important that you act professionally because you are representing yourself and your university.

Be prompt.	Late arrivals are not acceptable, so please arrive on-time.
Dress appropriately and professionally.	Maintain a professional appearance. If you have questions about dress, ask your supervisor.
Follow the schedule set by your supervisor.	Do not ask to leave early without a valid reason. Check with your supervisor ahead of time if you have an outstanding appointment that will result in your being late or leaving early. All coursework, employment, social commitments, and athletic commitments must not interfere with the responsibilities set by your field supervisor. You MUST make arrangements with your supervisor to make up ALL missed internship hours, including hours missed due to holidays, inclement weather, and illnesses.
Follow all policies.	Make yourself aware of and follow all policies associated with your internship placement, including those dealing with **confidentiality** and maintaining appropriate boundaries. Discuss any policy-related questions or concerns with your supervisor.
Be knowledgeable	Demonstrate an interest in the organization by understanding the goals and function, and demonstrate an active desire to learn and contribute.
Be patient	Be sensitive to the many demands that confront your supervisor and other office staff. They may not always be immediately available to respond to your questions or concerns. If needed, request an appointment with your supervisor to discuss any issue that is of concern to you.
Show respect	Show your supervisor and other office staff the respect they are due. Maintain a calm and respectful demeanor when discussing any concerns with your supervisor or other office staff. Do not disobey, insult, or in any other way be disrespectful to your supervisor or other office staff. If you disagree, please communicate your feelings in a constructive manner. Likewise, treat all clients in a respectful manner.
Be flexible and open to suggestions and self- evaluation.	Your internship provides you with a set of learning opportunities. You can demonstrate your appreciation for this educational opportunity by *remaining flexible and open to suggestions.* In particular, be willing to assist with clerical tasks such as filing, reception duties, and copying. You should not be expected to assume full-time responsibility for these tasks, but it is anticipated that you will assist with these tasks.
Work on Interpersonal Skills	Communicate with your supervisor, colleagues and community members effectively verbally and in writing. Be willing to ask others for help if needed. In doing so, demonstrate your willingness to establish rapport within the agency and community. Be mindful of issues of diversity.
Understand your Limits	You are completing an internship as partial fulfillment of your B.S. degree. You do not hold a 4 year degree or specialized certification, so you must recognize when tasks you are given are inappropriate.

Complete tasks on time	Check your work before submitting it to your supervisor and make sure that it is organized.
Take appropriate initiative	Supervisors appreciate interns taking appropriate initiative. If you finish a task early, ask for another assignment or develop a task. Make sure that your initiatives do not violate internship site policies. If in doubt, check with your supervisor.

Student Signature   _____

Internship Supervisor's Signature   _____

University Internship Supervisor   _____

We advise that you review this with all parties and complete during the first week of your internship.

REFERENCES

Coombes, B. (2009). Generation Y: Are they really digital natives or more like digital refugees. *Synergy, 7*(1), 31–40.

Kolb, D. A., Boyatzis, R. E., & Mainemelis, C. (2001). Experiential learning theory: Previous research and new directions. *Perspectives on thinking, learning, and cognitive styles, 1,* 227–247.

Parilla, P. F., & Hesser, G. W. (1998). Internships and the sociological perspective: Applying principles of experiential learning. *Teaching Sociology, 26*(4): 310–329.

Slick, G.A. (2000) Communication: The key to successful field experiences, Thousand Oaks, CA: Corwin Press.

5 Walking the Walk
Learning to Act Like a Professional

OBJECTIVES

- ➤ Describe the relationship between first impressions and professional outcomes
- ➤ Generate professional self-presentation in person
- ➤ Assemble appropriate attire for an interview and during an internship
- ➤ Create appropriate boundaries in professional interactions using ethical considerations
- ➤ Interact with potential internship sites and employers using person-first language, non-heterosexist, culturally sensitive language

Our department recently began requiring all majors to participate in an internship as a means of providing a structural mechanism through which students could build their career-related skills, begin to engage in their professional communities, and begin establishing their professional networks. During this transition, the Internship Coordinator (Dr. Kozak) initiated an Internship Fair, in which community agencies could interact with undergraduates to assess the pool of potential interns, but also as a means for interns to practice their professional behaviors.

We assumed that students understood the importance of self-presentation to potential internship sites, and therefore no additional instructions were given to them other than to make every effort to attend the Internship Fair if they were seeking an internship within the next two semesters. During the first Internship Fair, potential interns arrived in casual clothes, similar to those they would wear to class, with their backpacks in tow, and very few brought resumes to share with the internship site representatives.

We were astounded that what seemed like common knowledge to us wasn't even a consideration for our students. As a result, Dr. Kozak primed the students for the next Internship Fair, informing them that they were going to engage with people active in the field they planned to enter. Students were encouraged to present themselves in business casual clothes and come prepared with their resumes (see Chapter 3 for resume information).

Representatives from the internship sites who had attended both Internship Fairs provided unsolicited comments to Dr. Kozak on the difference between the two cohorts of students. Specifically, internship site representatives mentioned that the second cohort of students were much more professional in appearance, much more prepared to discuss their internship goals and ideas, and more aware of the internship sites in terms of mission of the organization and potential opportunities for interns. This example only provides anecdotal evidence based on a small sample of internship sites and students; it however illustrates the necessity of paying attention to first impressions across a wide array of experiences and environments.

There appears to be a gap in communicating the importance of a first impression and professionalism to students. Perhaps because what professors and employers think is common sense with regard to professionalism comes from experience over time or is so ingrained in them that it's overlooked in mentoring new professionals. The result is a new generation of professionals lacking the information on how to behave in their chosen profession in terms of self-presentation and interacting with other professionals, particularly those in supervisory positions. Therefore, we intend to rectify this oversight through specific attention to professional behaviors, self-presentation in person and in writing, through your manner of dress, through ethical interactions with coworkers, and through awareness of issues of diversity in a professional setting.

COMMUNICATING WHO YOU ARE IN PERSON

How many of you have experienced sitting in front of your screen, just watching the cursor blink, mocking your attempts to get just the right phrasing! Humans feel the strong need to create meaning in writing when we don't have access to the ability to communicate non-verbally or the ability to interpret the non-verbal messages of the receiver. Why, you ask? Humans are wired to look for universal cues in body posture, facial expression, and tone of voice that have meaning for everyone. In fact, these nonverbal behaviors constitute the overwhelming majority of the messages we send, so we feel at a loss when they aren't available to us. For example, approximately 55% of what you say is transmitted through face and body positions and 38% of your message is conveyed through vocal qualities such as tone of voice, pitch, and volume (Griffin, 1998). Do the math and you realize that 93% of your total in-person message is transmitted through non-verbal means, thus leaving you frustrated by a blinking cursor and creating fertile ground for misunderstandings through text or emails.

Important face and body positions to consider. Most of you have learned the importance of the handshake. Aim for a firm, but not crushing, handshake *with one or two hand pumps. While you can't do much about the temperature of your hands*, you can create the opportunity for them to be reasonably dry by sitting with your palms up in a relaxed hand position on your lap. By doing so, you won't have a hot sweaty handshake for your interview or when meeting important professional contacts. A side benefit is that this hand position conveys honesty and openness, so it's a win-win!

Non-verbal postures such as sitting and body positioning have meaning in the professional world as well. For example, rushing to sit down conveys nervousness, while sitting with your head slightly tilted suggests that you are listening intently and are interested in what the speaker is saying. Nodding tells the speaker that you are following along as they are speaking, similar to what a tilted head conveys. Use this judiciously, however, because if you overuse it and look like a bobble-head, you can seem submissive and obsequious.

Lastly, a slightly thrust out chin can convey confidence, but be careful as this might be interpreted as arrogance. The pictures in 5.1 illustrate the difference in how we interpret body position based solely on posture. What impressions do you have of Figure 5.1a in contrast to those of Figure 5.1b? As you can see, simple awareness of how your body positions are interpreted by others can benefit you in making first impressions or in your interactions with coworkers and supervisors during your internship.

Vocal qualities. As noted earlier, vocal qualities come in second place in terms of conveying information to others. While some of you are thinking, "I can't control the pitch of my voice," we encourage you to think about the ways you moderate your vocal qualities according to whom you are speaking. For example, how do you speak to your dog or cat? What about to a baby? Your significant other? A parent? A colleague? Say something out loud in the tone of voice you would normally use with each of these. For some of you, they might be identical, but it is far more likely that most, if not all, of you used different tones of voice for each. In fact, adults speak to infants in such a consistent manner that it has been dubbed 'Mom-ese.'

We suggest to those with high, child-like voices to practice pitching your voice a little lower than you would ordinarily use. Even those with moderately pitched voices could practice using a slightly lower voice because humans unconsciously increase their vocal pitch when they are nervous or anxious, which you are likely to be during an interview or at the beginning of your internship.

Similarly, we typically speed up our speech when nervous, so practice speaking slowly and clearly before interacting with potential internship supervisors or officers. Volume plays a role as well, so speak loudly enough to be heard but make sure you aren't yelling or overpowering others. Lastly, there is a tendency of this generation of students to end sentences on a rising note which sounds like the speaker is unsure and asking a question. Not only does it convey that you lack confidence, but many persons in positions of authority (read: supervisors) find this particular tendency annoying and think it makes the speaker sound immature and sophomoric—not the impression you want your internship supervisor to have of you!

FIGURE 5.1

Verbals. Though the majority of this section has been about the importance of nonverbal behaviors and their connection to internships, the authors believe there are a few in-person verbal issues worthy of note. For example, avoid using vocal fillers when speaking to potential internship sites, supervisors, community members, or constituents of your internship organization. Vocal fillers are phrases such as ummm, like, you know, you know what I mean, literally, seriously, totally, etc. A verbal filler such as 'and so forth' conveys you don't really know or understand the details. Be specific, yet concise, about details and avoid using this phrase unless you are using it to skip over a portion of your story or report what is already known to the listener.

Finally, it is best to avoid tentative language when attempting to secure an internship or even during your internship experience. Tentative language is similar to both the nonverbal behaviors and verbal qualities discussed earlier that convey lack of confidence and/or insecurity. Examples of tentative language used in person and in writing with suggestions about how to rephrase them are included in Table 5.1.

TABLE 5.1. Tentative language and their fixes.

Tentative Language	Confident language
Sort of/Kind of	Avoid using these; directly state your idea or results
I was just thinking	Based on what we've done before, I think Based on what's been effective previously, X can help us… Using X as an example, I've think Y is the best solution.
I was just writing to let you know…	As a follow-up to our conversation this morning, I am/have…
I am planning to…	In order to meet the goals we've discussed, I am….
I'm sorry	Use this **only** when actually apologizing for a mistake (see Not Sorry video in References)

DRESSING FOR THE PART

The Internship Fair anecdote earlier in the chapter illustrates the importance of self-presentation through attire. In our department, students prepare to dress for future employment through the professional development course. We use guest lecturers from the Fashion Merchandising program, during which students are asked to wear something they would wear to an interview. In

the course of this guest lecture, students learn how to tailor their choices depending upon the environments in which they will be interning, and they are given suggestions on how to alter their selections during their internship. For example, students who plan to intern in a hospital or a school setting are likely to wear similar clothes to an interview as they would during their internship (provided they won't be wearing scrubs). Conversely, students who are interning with a local farm-to-school program might wear professional clothes to an interview but need to wear more casual clothes during their actual internship.

Unfortunately, not all programs include instruction on how to dress appropriately in their curriculum. In fact, we receive texts and emails regularly from colleagues who tell us about wardrobe infractions made by millennials in their offices. Examples include trapeze dresses that float upwards when rushing down a hallway late for a meeting (two infractions: being late *and* inappropriately dressed), or too-high platforms worn during a presentation that have participants noticing the presenter's awkward gait rather than the content. Though there are many references easily searchable on the Internet, not all students have been instructed to look for this invaluable information.

In preparation for this chapter, Dr. Gonyea informally polled colleagues across multiple disciplines (College Administration, nonprofit agencies, public service, education, public health, graduate education programs, etc.). The responses received are summarized in *The basics of professional dress*. There are a few items on the list that deserve some clarification. For example, you should check your hemlines when sitting, standing, bending, and so forth. While this often applies to women and skirt length, it is also appropriate for men. Even though the implication is different when a woman's skirt is too high or when a man's trouser leg rides too high and shows a hairy leg, the end result is the same. In both instances, it is assumed that the person in the too-short clothing has a low degree of professionalism; a supervisor is less likely to give that person choice assignments, to have that person interact with other key persons, or to allow that person to represent the organization to the community (Haefner, 2008; Lorenz, 2008). Similarly, clothing that is too tight (for both men and women) makes the wearer look unkempt, unmotivated, and in general, as though they don't care about the internship. The resulting impression on supervisors is that the student doesn't value the internship.

Pay attention to the tasks that you will be assigned during your internship in terms of hemlines and necklines as well. For example, a draped neck blouse for women might be fine for someone whose main task involves sitting in front of a computer. However, for interns working with small children and who are likely to spend a greater part of their day sitting in a miniature chair, sitting criss-cross-applesauce on the floor, squatting down to a three-year olds' eye level, or bent at the waist, perhaps skirts in general and drape neck shirts aren't good choices.

Let's talk about hair for a moment—another issue of equal importance for men and women. Each generation of female college students has a 'go to' hairstyle for class, for example, a fountain, a sock bun, or a messy pony. Often born out of functionality and the need to get ready quickly or stand up to windy treks across campus, these are not universally appropriate for the workplace. When a student arrives for class dressed for an interview or a presentation, we often do a double take because the chosen hairstyle is so different from their everyday look. Specific to hair for men is the issue of facial hair. If wild and wooly beards are in style, make sure that you keep yours well-groomed for your internship. If you have a moustache or mutton chops, they can be as wild as you would like in your personal time, but keep it cleaned up during your internship. Body hair other than your face should either be covered by your professional clothes or removed altogether.

Another unisex issue is that of hats. For men, athletic hats that cover a balding spot or just represent your fandom just aren't appropriate for an internship. The one exception might be an internship in a placement where the bulk of your time is spent outside and the hat is necessary for sun protection, shade, or other important functions. Fashion hats, such as a fedora or a newsboy, can be worn depending upon your specific internship site. Make sure you pay attention to the culture of the organization before wearing hats in general.

© 2016 by mikrop. Used under licesne from Shutterstock, Inc.

© 2016 by Gokce Gurellier. Used under license from Shutterstock, Inc.

Scent is included on the list, despite the lack of agreement on whether or not scent is appropriate for the workplace. Interestingly, the two sexes differ in their evaluation of perfume in the workplace. Men rate potential employees who wear perfume in the workplace lower than that of their scentless peers. Conversely, women are more likely to rate the potential employees wearing scent higher than those without scent (Baron, 1983). Additional research indicates that applicants who wear more stereotypically masculine scents are more likely to be employed than those who wear stereotypically feminine scents (Sczesney & Stahlberg, 2002).

Lastly, body decorations such as tattoos and piercings are often specifically prohibited in the workplace. If they aren't specifically mentioned in an employee handbook or your site doesn't have an employee or intern handbook, a good rule of thumb is to keep these covered or take them out while you are onsite. These guidelines apply to employment after graduation as well.

Millennials have been socialized differently from preceding generations of Generation X, and Baby Boomers. As such, they are more likely to want to dress casually, have lower levels of formality (Cardon & Okoro, 2009), and have been parented in a way that emphasizes being "younique" (Behrens, 2009, p. 21) more so than their bosses/supervisors. Even though they report wanting to dress more casually, Millennials also report feeling the most authoritative, trustworthy, and competent when wearing more formal attire (Peluchette & Karl, 2007). While they also feel the most friendly and creative when they wear more casual clothes (Peluchette & Karl, 2007), these qualities though important, are related less to the likelihood of advancement, increased

---

The basics of professional dress

No wrinkles

Casual Friday doesn't mean sloppy or ripped

Casual Friday doesn't apply when you have office visitors, meetings outside the office, or are presenting

Hemlines no more than two inches above the knee

Necklines—no cleavage, no shoulders, no draping

No club dresses or short skirts

Platforms are 'fun' shoes, not office shoes

No button-downs that gape between buttons

No 'straps' (bra straps, cami straps, tank tops, etc) showing

Nothing so tight we can see your undergarments

Nothing so loose we can see your undergarments

No strong perfume/cologne

Well-groomed hair (face, body, or head)

Attire that is appropriate to your tasks

No flip flops

Leggings/Tights are not pants

No midriff baring shirts

No low rise pants unless shirts are tucked

No message Ts

No political or cause related messages on clothing

Avoid distracting jewelry (bangles that make noise when you move/type; oversized earrings)

Simple is best!

compensation, and perceptions of success. In addition, dressing professionally gives you more credibility and creates the impression that you take your responsibilities seriously (*Professional Pointers*, 2005).

The generational differences in views about workplace attire is particularly relevant to professional behaviors, because Millennnials are much more likely to think that their more casual attire and familiar behaviors are acceptable, despite the fact that their supervisors are likely to be from a different generation where this is a sign of immaturity or lack of confidence. In fact, Behrens (2009) notes that those hiring Millennials need to provide, or be prepared to provide, a rationale for why employees can't have tattoos showing or why they can't wear more revealing clothes.

The bottom line is that it doesn't matter how *you* feel about the way you present yourself, but it matters to the person you are trying to make an impression upon. Some of you might argue, 'this is the real me and if they don't like it, it isn't the place I should be working.' However, being the 'real you' doesn't matter until you have some clout. After you have built social capital in your field, you will have much more flexibility in how you present yourself because you will have some history. At that point, your colleagues, employers, and the community will know the quality of your work, and are less likely to judge you based on their preconceived notions about things like body art.

Your goal is to look respectable but not boring (Belkin, 2004). For Millennials, this means finding a way to balance demonstrating your personality with the need to be professional. Using these examples in Figure 5.2, how would you rate the professionalism in their versions of casual and corporate business attire? Casual work environment attire allows the wearer some latitude through color, prints, accessories, and so forth. We would critique the attire in Figure 5.2a as being too much cleavage for the workplace, especially as an intern. However, the images for a more corporate work environment hit the mark—respectable but not boring. Here too there is some personality shown through accessories, however, the outfits inspire confidence, look polished, and look professional.

FIGURE 5.2

Business casual

(a)

(b)

(c)

Corporate attire

(d)

(e)

(f)

Professional Interpersonal Boundaries

We can all agree that the email example at the beginning of this chapter demonstrated poor professional boundaries. Sometimes it is very clear where to draw the line between your personal life and your professional one, yet other times the line is less distinct. Interns exist in the no-man's land of not-employee and not-student, therefore are especially susceptible to blurred boundaries. Consider this: as an intern you are constantly being evaluated, and therefore might be less likely to tell a supervisor 'no' even when you know the task is wrong or suspect it might be inappropriate for an intern.

Unfortunately, these situations occur during internships frequently enough for us to address them here. For instance, an intern was asked to drive clients of a state-funded organization in her personal vehicle in order to transport them to an event held by the organization. The intern realized that this was an inappropriate task because: a) it puts the intern at risk by being alone with clients; b) it puts the organization at risk for the same reason; c) the vehicle was her own personal property; and d) the intern had not been approved to drive clients in any vehicle much less her own. Despite understanding that the task was inappropriate for an intern, she was hesitant to refuse because she was afraid that she would be evaluated poorly for not complying.

In addition, an intern was asked to sign off on services for a client of a federally funded organization for which the organization billed MediCare. This student was also in the difficult position of potentially receiving a poor evaluation; however, she decided to say something anyway. The intern handled the situation well by asking her onsite supervisor about the logistics of the organization, specifically how the organization was paid, types of service that were covered, and whether she, as an intern, was able to provide those services since she was still a student. When the supervisor told the intern that it was ok if she signed off on services as long as the supervisor also signed, the intern was still uncomfortable and went to her on-campus internship supervisor. Of course, the on-campus supervisor brought the concerns to the legal affairs division of the university, who reported the fraud to the appropriate agency. The result was a full-scale investigation of the agency for insurance fraud.

What other concerns might the intern have had outside of the worries about a negative evaluation? In this particular example, had the student not reported the issue to her on-campus supervisor, she could have been held legally responsible for the insurance fraud, practicing without a valid license, or even been at risk of being sued by the client or the client's family if anything had happened to that client. Ultimately, the student was not able to complete her internship at that particular site given the investigation of the organization for illegal behaviors, coupled with the poor quality of the supervision. Fortunately, the on-campus supervisor was able to secure a second placement for the intern such that she could complete her hours and her internship project. Unfortunately, the student had the opportunity to learn more during that internship than she would have liked to!

The above examples are as much about ethical decision making (to be covered in Chapter 7), as much as it is about the creation of appropriate workplace boundaries between your role as an intern and that of an employee of the organization. This chapter explores how interns can create appropriate boundaries in professional interactions using ethical considerations, more specifically, how interns can successfully establish boundaries between their work and personal lives, between themselves and their colleagues, and between themselves and those served by their internship site.

NSFW (Not Safe for Work)

A colleague recently wrote to us detailing an experience she had with a recent hire. Her coworkers are all recent Masters-level Fellows paid through a Federal grant. As new Fellows, all of them attend an orientation during which they learn about their fellowship, their responsibilities, and the expectations of the fellowship. The email said, "If I can see the word

'nipple' over your shoulder, it's not safe for work!" Apparently, the new Fellow was reading *50 Shades of Grey* on her tablet during the orientation. This behavior is problematic for numerable reasons: a) the Fellow will not know what is expected of her, therefore she will ask questions about things her supervisors expect her to already know; b) she is building a reputation for being uninterested, untrustworthy, and inappropriate; and c) she will have a more steep learning curve about her job, leading her coworkers and supervisors to think she is struggling or not competent.

While the content in this example might be extreme, we are inclined to believe it is a fairly common practice for Millennials to 'multi-task'—doing something digitally while engaged in an in-person meeting. It is fairly obvious to faculty that you are not taking notes on class content when you snicker, poke the person sitting next to you, and show them your laptop screen. If you are representing your internship site, ultimately you are responsible for anything missed, in addition to how you represent your internship site; therefore you should minimize the amount of 'multi-tasking' you do.

As noted earlier, Millennials are a much less formal generation and are much more likely to want or create a flattened hierarchy in their internships or in their careers. This tendency lends itself to teamwork and an increased sense of community at work (Dumas, Phillips, & Rothbard, 2013; Millet, 2003). The downside, however, is twofold. First, as mentioned in Chapter 2, there are blurred boundaries between professional life, personal life, and digital life which can lead to increased stress. Second, these indistinct boundaries and behaviors, when stressed, can make Millennials appear less professional in the eyes of their supervisors who are Gen Xers or Baby Boomers with an entirely different set of expectations.

Technology and Workplace Boundaries

Millennials and many current employees report an expectation of availability and responsiveness via technology in their workplaces. Interns must balance the flexibility of being available via technology and the potential for being abused. For example, mobile devices allow for increased flexibility in communication between interns and both their onsite and their faculty supervisors. While the benefits include the ability of interns to ask questions when not on campus or on site, confirm information or protocols, or submit logs, journals and reports, there is an inherent risk of being *too* available. Unless there are specific guidelines or expectations in place, it is very easy to slip into having poor boundaries around accessibility, leading to a potentially abusive situation where the intern is working much more than was outlined in the internship agreement or the supervisor requires much more of the intern than was agreed upon.

As an example, smartphones can be utilized as a tool to balance internship, school and personal life. In a study of how women use their mobile devices as a way to balance their work and home lives, women reported the expectation of availability and responsiveness. Some of the women reported difficulty turning it off, that it was "joined to me on my hip", and that they were sick in bed with the flu using a mobile device to communicate with the office even when "my body was aching to the point it hurts" (Crowe & Middleton, 2012, p. 564).

In order to avoid potential problems during your internship, we offer some suggestions for establishing a boundary with your internship site, especially when the onsite supervisor doesn't broach the topic. During your negotiations about the internship, you should talk to your onsite supervisor about their use of technology to understand the culture of the particular organization: do they use particular apps or software; do they use text messaging to communicate with one another during work hours? What about during non-work hours? Are there time ranges when it is unacceptable to text or message someone? Also, what are the expectations of you, as an intern, in terms of your use of technology: e.g. what is the expected turnaround time for you to respond via email, text, or phone call? Should you respond in the same way you were contacted (e.g. respond to texts with texts, respond via phone to an email, etc.)?

You might suggest to your onsite supervisor that the organization establish an email associated with your internship site rather than making you use your personal or university email. Related to this, you can establish times that you are available and will be responsive to emails, texts, or calls, as well as when you are not available (e.g. during on-campus class times, etc). Some internships will expect you to always be available during the hours you allocated to your internship; however, depending on your internship, there might be times you are not available such as during meetings, while conducting a community program, or other such events. Establishing times you are and are not available, both during your internship hours and outside of them, accomplishes two goals. First, you understand what is expected of you during your internship. Second, by setting the boundary at the outset, you prevent stress associated with being 'on-call' 24/7, as well as protect your time to accomplish other tasks, related to your internship or other courses in which you may be enrolled.

Lastly, depending on your internship site, there may be potential confidentiality issues related to your use of technology. Ask about your internship site's policy regarding confidential information (e.g. identifying information about customers/clients) and ask how to handle this type of confidential information should you need to use emails or texting to discuss internship-related information. While we suggest asking about this during negotiations of your intern contract or Memorandum of Understanding (MOU: legal contract between your university and your internship site), if in doubt, err on the side of caution and ethical behavior by **not** including identifying information about your internship at all.

Boundaries between you and your colleagues

Interns have one foot in their university, where they have a proscribed role as a student with specific role responsibilities and expectations, and the other in the role of an employee, where their role might be more open to interpretation. Employees may have more flexible standards for interactions among co-workers and the flattened hierarchy noted earlier. The act of dual citizenship in these two environments might lead interns to gravitate toward the more casual set of boundaries.

At first glance, casual workplace boundaries don't appear to be a problem. However, for interns who are being constantly evaluated and who are expected to be building a professional network, this can be problematic. For example, many of our alumni have found employment through their internship experiences resulting in former students supervising current students in their internship sites. On the surface, this situation works for everyone: our alumni have found jobs in their field through their internships and our current students can work with students they either know personally or who have a good working knowledge of disciplinary content and skills. However, as detailed in Chapter 2, there are significant drawbacks to poor boundaries between you (personal life) and your coworkers (professional life).

Being friends with a supervisor means that you are much more likely to take their evaluation of you or your work personally. Perhaps you socialize outside of work and they have met your significant other or your children. Perhaps you expect your supervisor to understand non-work stressors in your life and how these might affect your work product. After all, they *know* you. Unfortunately, when we receive declining evaluations of acceptance (negative evaluations from friends), we are much more likely to be hurt and to have our self-esteem be negatively affected (Buckley et al., 2004). As a result, workplace relationships are then strained, leading to increased stress, poor evaluation of the work environment, and ultimately poor performance.

Consider also the supervisor's perspective. In the example given above, alumni who are now supervising current students in their internships are ultimately responsible for the work product associated with the internship. They are also responsible for their own work, the way the intern and the organization is represented to other community agencies, service providers, and consumers, and their reputation among all of these. While it may seem really attractive to be supervised by a former classmate, the alum has much more investment as an employee and is likely to have a different set of expectations of your performance than he or she would have had as a fellow student.

Boundaries between you and those served by your internship

The last area of consideration for boundary development during an internship is that of those built between you and the families or individuals with whom you work. Generally speaking, Family Science internships involve working directly with individuals and families with the intention of improving lives, conditions, or skills. Due to the nature of Family Science direct service and the personality traits that lead students to choose this field, many of our interns find it difficult *not* to make connections and build relationships with those they meet through their internship. The task of creating appropriate boundaries around your work (i.e. leaving it 'at the office') takes practice and experience; thus, this text will focus on creating boundaries between your personal views and the views of those whom you are working with or serving.

Boundaries around biases. Most Family Science internship placements will address at least one of the inherently value-laden National Council on Family Relations [NCFR] Content Areas (NCFR, 2011: See Chapter 4 for matrix substance areas). These content areas span all areas of human development and family functioning and represent contentious content in terms of the values and opinions associated with them. For example, there are strong opinions about discipline in Parent Education and Guidance, about talking to children about sex in Human Sexuality, and about same-sex relationships in Interpersonal Relationships. How do you maintain the three-way distinction between your own values about what you think *should be,* what actually *is* for individuals and families served by your internship, and research that tells you *what works?* This text began with an exploration of your personal identity and biases in order to help you develop ways to distinguish between your beliefs and your role as an effective intern. In order to do so, you will need to understand your own thinking and belief systems and how these can impact your work during your internship.

You are more likely to be able to create a boundary between your own views and opinions when focusing on the role you are taking during your internship. For example, your own opinions matter little if your primary function is to impart information based on research or as part of a pre-packaged program. While your own lenses are apt to emerge in *how* you impart the information and which information you choose to emphasize, your essential function is to impart the program information. Therefore, to be an effective intern, you should concentrate on the facts. This doesn't remove the human tendency to form opinions about the people with whom we work, but it does set limits for your actions while on your internship. Also, we would encourage you to understand how negative or alienating interactions between you and your program participants would actually be counterproductive to your goals of improving lives: if they don't participate or aren't engaged because they feel judged, they will not benefit from the program.

Person-first language

Say This:	Not This:
Same-sex couples	Homosexual couples
Different-sex couples	Heterosexual couples
Person with [insert appropriate term] Examples: Teen with Down's Syndrome, Child with Albinism	Disabled Handicapped
Partners	Husband or Wife
Immigrant families Non-nationals Persons from [country of origin]	Illegal Aliens Illegals Foreigners
Divorced or separated families	Broken families Broken homes

Related to the awareness of and attention to boundaries around biases, interns should be aware of the language they use when interacting with community members, internship supervisors and coworkers, or persons served by their internship. The accepted standard in any Family Science related field, whether intern, supervisor, or faculty member, is person-first language. Person-first language reflects an understanding that we are *people* before we are the *qualities* that we possess. This is a strengths-based way of acknowledging difference while putting the humanity of an individual before their group affiliation. Person-first language demonstrates cultural sensitivity (a.k.a. cultural competence), gender-neutrality, non-heterosexism, and sensitivity to community needs and values according to the NCFR Content Areas (NCFR, 2011) and the ethical values espoused by the organization (Alden, Cassidy, Cooke, & Palm, 2009).

Boundaries around emotions. Often the issue at hand is not that of unintentional bias toward participants, but rather that of feeling protective or connected to them. It is incredibly difficult to remain unmoved when you see others hurting. As noted earlier, resolving how best to maintain appropriate emotional boundaries takes practice over time. It is unlikely that there is sufficient time to become an expert in creating appropriate emotional boundaries within a semester-long internship; however, there are some steps you can take to begin the process.

First, you should know your limits about emotional content and stress. An internship is already a potentially stressful time when you are asked to broaden your thinking, work differently from how you have been working as a student, and perhaps need to learn how to balance internship duties and continued coursework. By consistently evaluating where you are with regard to your stress level (see Chapter 1 for assessment), you are more likely to know when you are approaching your emotional limits and will be able to create a plan to diffuse the situation before it becomes problematic or too overwhelming.

Inherent in knowing your limits is an understanding of self-regulation. What are your favorite strategies for reducing an emotional load or de-stressing and are they healthy coping strategies? For example, do you practice mindfulness or engage in physical activity in order to release emotional energy? Or are you likely to engage in less healthy behaviors that might be temporarily effective, but take a toll in the long run? Obviously, we would advocate for the healthier alternatives to self-regulation and encourage you to develop additional coping strategies prior to your internship so that you have more to draw upon should you need them.

A healthy method of self-regulation is creating a habit of appropriate self-care prior to beginning your internship. Though there are many methods, some that might be helpful to you as you prepare for your internship are:

> Create an interns peer support group online for your intern cohort
> Schedule down-time at key points in the week
> Schedule time for friends during your internship
> Get enough sleep
> Practice healthy eating habits
> Do not make major life transitions during your internship
> Plan times when you are available to your internship site
> Keep on track with other assignments/courses so you don't fall behind
> Schedule wisely—space out emotionally difficult events over the week, plan to have re-charging activities between them

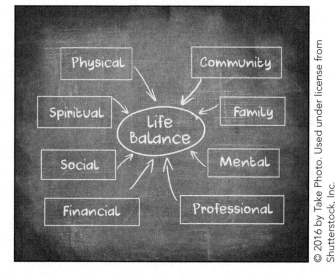

© 2016 by Take Photo. Used under license from Shutterstock, Inc.

Lastly, develop a professional relationship with either your onsite supervisor or your on-campus supervisor. By choosing an appropriate professional relationship with either of these individuals, you can create a space during your internship where you can process the experience, either in person or through your logs/journals about your internship. Be mindful of not using this relationship for therapy or other personal growth, but rather develop the ability to effectively process your emotional reactions to your internship experiences. This accomplishes two goals. First, it provides you with the foundation for creating emotional boundaries with people you work with, as well as demonstrates to your supervisors that you are aware of and are working toward healthy boundaries within a safe, structured environment.

Boundaries around behaviors. The example of the student who was asked to use her personal vehicle to transport persons being served by her internship earlier in the chapter is an exceptional circumstance. The most common concern we hear from interns about problems with boundaries is with being offered gifts, especially among interns who work with children. Parents are socialized into buying gifts for most of the individuals who work with their children. Some examples include holiday or end-of-year presents for teachers and gifts for coaches, music, and dance instructors. They extend this to other service providers for their children, including when it is expressly forbidden, such as therapists, social workers, Child Life Specialists, and yes, even the interns with a child-based organization.

There are several considerations when thinking about receiving gifts from children or families with whom you work. First, whether or not your profession or your internship site expressly forbids it, accepting gifts is not a good idea. Yet, sometimes refusing the gift can be harmful to the relationship you've developed with the child or the family. So, what is an intern to do?

First, you should evaluate the value of the gift. If it is a hand-drawn picture from a child you work with, the monetary value is small, but the intent of the child is priceless, and therefore you can accept the gift. Some professions stipulate an estimated cutoff for gifts, under which you can accept them. Even in this instance, you should clear it with your internship before accepting the gift.

Gifts such as baked goods have limited market value; however, they should still be handled with care. One strategy for responding to this type of gift is to let the giver know that you will be sharing them with the entire staff in your break room. By doing so, you accept the gift graciously, maintain the relationship with the giver, and reduce any potential for taking advantage of the individuals with whom you work during your internship. Other types of handmade gifts, like hand-knitted scarves or other craft items, can be tricky. It isn't possible to share them, they have limited market value, and obviously the giver put time and energy into its creation. If you are interning in an environment that expressly forbids accepting gifts, you could let the giver know about the policy but offer to donate the item to an individual or family that needs it. In environments where gifts are not expressly forbidden, you could likely accept the item, but make sure to clear it with your supervisor before taking such an item home.

Regardless of the value of the gift, it is important to evaluate the impact that accepting or refusing the gift will have on your relationship with the giver. This depends largely on the roles and responsibilities of your internship. If you only interact with constituents in a large group setting during an educational program, you are less likely to offend or alienate someone by graciously refusing gifts of value. You are also much less likely to encounter this situation in those settings. However, in settings where you work closely with one person or family, work in their homes as a part of a community-based program, or in intense environments like a hospital setting, you are much more likely to have strong contacts, thus more likely to be offered a gift. In these circumstances, refer back to the issue of value, policy in your internship, and checking with your supervisor if unsure. When faced with this situation, it is sometimes better to accept the gift to maintain the relationship and then bring it to your supervisor's notice, than to attempt to navigate the situation yourself in the moment. Your supervisor then bears the responsibility of returning the gift if it is truly inappropriate, thereby maintaining your relationship with the individual or family.

APPLYING YOUR KNOWLEDGE

FIGURE 5.3

(a)

© 2015 by bikeriderlondon. Used under license of Shutterstock, Inc.

(b)

© 2015 by lev radin. Used under license of Shutterstock, Inc.

(c)

© 2015 by Dmitry Melnikov. Used under license of Shutterstock, Inc.

1. Imagine that you are an intern in a community-based afterschool program and the child in Figure 5.3a is a participant.
a. What are your immediate reactions to this person?
b. What assumptions do you make about him, his parents, his home life, his intelligence, and his activity level?
c. How might these assumptions affect your interactions with him?
d. What are the potential consequences for the child or the family as a result of your interactions with him?

2. Now, imagine that you intern at an alternative high school and the person in Figure 5.3b is one of your mentees.

a. What are your initial reactions/thoughts about this student?

b. How might your initial reactions/thoughts impact your interactions with this student?

c. What other information do you *need* in order to be a successful and effective mentor for this student?

d. What might this student interpret as your reactions and how might this influence your ability to be effective in your role as mentor?

3. Lastly, picture yourself as an intern for a parenting education program for young adult women. While at your friends' softball game at a local park, you see one of the soon-to-be moms from your internship in Figure 5.3c.

a. What is your initial reaction to seeing the pregnant woman drinking and smoking?

b. What are the parameters around your ability to interact with this person? Are you bound by confidentiality at your internship site and unable to acknowledge the woman?

c. What is your response or reaction when you encounter this person during your internship and how might she interpret your response to her?

4. Review both the Satterly image and the Life Map you created in Chapter 1 to remind yourself of your biases and their influences on your cultural competency. Reflecting on these, ask yourself the essential question: what is my role during my internship? List as many potential roles as you can think of that you might have during your internship. Examples include:
   - Imparting information
   - Developing and/or implementing a community program
   - Evaluating an existing community program
   - Creating opportunities for change in family systems
   - Developing informational materials for an organization

5. Using the space below, explore the potential ways your own biases might be activated during your internship.

REFERENCES

Alden, A., Cassidy, D., Cooke, B., & Palm, G. (2009). *Ethical thinking and practice for Family Life Educators.* Minnesota Council on Family Relations.

Bailey, E. (2010). *Writing and speaking at work (5ᵗʰ Ed.).* Prentice Hall: Paramus, NJ.

Baron, R. (1983). "Sweet smell of success"?: The impact of pleasant artificial scents on evaluations of job applicants. *Journal of Applied Psychology, 68(4),* 709–713.

Behrens, W. (2009). Managing Millennials: They're coming to a workplace near you. *Managing Health Services, Spring,* 19–21.

Belkin, L. (April 11, 2004). Fine line of dressing with a job in mind. New York Times, pp W1.

Buckley, K. E., Winkel, R. E., Leary, M. R. (2004). Reactions to acceptance and rejection: Effects of level and sequence of relational evaluation. *Journal of Experimental social Psychology, 40,* 14–28.

Cardon, P. & Okoro, E. (2009). Professional Characteristics Conveyed By Formal Versus Casual Workplace Attire. *Business Communication Quarterly, September,* 355–360.

Crowe, R. & Middleton, C. (2012). Women, smartphones, and the workplace. *Feminist Media Studies, 12(4),* 560–569.

Dumas, T., Phillips, K., & Rothbard, N. (2013). Getting closer at the company party: Integration experiences, racial dissimilarity, and workplace relationships. *Organization Science,* 1377–1401.

Griffin, J. (1998). *How to Say it at Work.* Prentice Hall: Paramus, NJ.

Haefner, R. (2009, July 30). *How to dress for success for work.* Retrieved from http://www.cnn.com/2008/LIVING/worklife/07/30/cb.dress.for.success/index.html

Joseph, L. (January 7, 2014). 7 Email writing skills that many business professionals ignore. Retrieved from https://www.udemy.com/blog/email-writing-skills/

Lorenz, (2009, July 25). *Do you dress for success?* Retrieved from http://www.careerbuilder.com/Article/CB-929-The-Workplace-Do-You-Dress-for-Success/

Millet, S. (2003). A Product Of Social Interaction: Tag Team Reference And Workplace Relationships. *The Reference Librarian, 83–84,* 23–31. Doi: 10.1300J120v40n83_03

National Council on Family Relations. (2011). *Family Life Education Content Areas.*

Not Sorry [Video file]. Retrieved from https://www.youtube.com/watch?v=rzL-vdQ3ObA

Paglieri, J. (December 12, 2014). The Sony Mega-hack: What you need to know. Retrieved from http://money.cnn.com/2014/12/09/technology/security/sony-hacking-roundup/

Peluchette, J. & Karl, K. (2007). The impact of workplace attire on employee self-perceptions. *Human Resource Development Quarterly, 18(3),* 345–360.

Professional Pointers. (April, 2005). Dress the Part. *Teller Vision.* Aspen Publishers, Inc. p. 5.

Sczesney, S. & Stahlberg, D. (2002). The influence of gender stereotyped perfumes of leadership attribution. *European Journal of Social Psychology, 32 (6),* 815–828.

Wade, L. (August 26, 2014). 10 Things every college professor hates. Business Insider. Retrieved from http://www.businessinsider.com/10-things-every-college-professor-hates-2014-8?IR=T&

6 Setting the Tone in Your Interview

OBJECTIVES

➤ Produce a strategy for getting an internship interview
➤ Create a plan for researching the organization before the interview
➤ Explain the process of interviewing for an internship
➤ Differentiate between the qualities of 'good' versus 'bad' interviews
➤ Demonstrate responses to likely interview questions
➤ Discriminate between inappropriate interview questions and illegal interview questions
➤ Appraise your own interview readiness

Judging by the feedback offered by our students over multiple semesters, interviews for internships take many different forms, ranging from very formal interviews with cohort model internship programs to informal, casual conversations over a cup of coffee. Regardless of the level of formality of your internship interview, the interview is an intricate dance between you and the interviewer in which you attempt to read and decode signals back and forth while also encoding and sending signals about your qualifications, goals, and capabilities. You must be able to read signals correctly in order for the interview to progress at an easy, relaxed pace, which is the hallmark of a good interview. No matter what the structure of your interview is, your task is to sell your qualifications and credibility to your potential employers while determining if the internship site will be able to meet your professional development and academic needs. To do so, there are at least two agendas that you need to focus on during an interview, and potentially up to four: your agenda, the interviewers' agenda, your hidden agenda, and the interviewers' hidden agenda (DeLuca & DeLuca, 2001).

Your agenda should be based on what you want the interviewer to learn about you by the end of your conversation. Determine the main points you want to make about yourself, your accomplishments, your goals, and how the organization would benefit from having you as an intern. Also, your agenda should include a list of the types of information you want to gather about your internship site. For example, you may want to ascertain the culture of the organization in terms of dress code, technology use, morale, level of oversight, quality of the supervision and then evaluate if these match your expectations or needs for your internship. Your *hidden* agenda may include a need to prove that you can get offered the internship even if it isn't your first choice of placement, and is perhaps only a backup. In addition, you may be discreetly evaluating whether or not the internship site is able to provide you with the types of supervision you need for your program. You may also be checking to see whether or not you will be able to gain the types of experiences you would like for your professional development or if you will get the number of hours you need to meet departmental or other regulatory board requirements. For example, our interns are required to conduct 40 clock hours per credit of internship course credit (240 clock hours for 6 credit hours of internship) and use this as a screening tool for selecting an internship site.

We address self-presentations skills in Chapter 5 and strongly recommend that you review the sections on presenting yourself in writing and in person before interviewing for your internship. However, this section is devoted specifically to interviewing, so that regardless of the formality or structure of your interview, you will be prepared for it. Specifically, in this chapter you will learn how to get interviews; conduct self-assessments of your skills and characteristics to help you educate the interviewer on why you are a good fit with their organization; learn how to use the self assessments in preparing to be interviewed; understand the interview process; and learn what to ask and what **not** to ask.

GETTING THE INTERVIEW

Interviewing for an internship or a job requires that you create an image, or a brand, that represents who you are and what you bring to the company or organization. While that might sound intimidating to some and perhaps a somewhat too corporate a perspective to apply to Family Science, you have already learned the basics of creating your brand through exploration of your identity and understanding your digital identity in the first two chapters.

Getting an interview and advancement in your career are founded upon the relationships you develop with your peers, your supervisors, and your colleagues, therefore when you begin to look for an internship site, you should start with your current network. An obvious place to start looking for an interview is through organizations in which you already volunteer and that are related to your career goals. This is a good place to start, however we want to strongly encourage you to use those conversations as jumping off point to explore other opportunities. Many students are the most flexible with the least number of ties to one place than at any other time in their lives. Being competitive in the job market means having a wide range of experiences and skills. If you stay at an organization for your internship are you going to be doing more of the same? Will you be able to add skills, experiences, or new leadership to your resume? If not, then it will be better for you in the long run to explore other opportunities to increase your marketability after graduation.

If you aren't currently volunteering (and you should be!), meet with faculty members who teach relevant subjects or are working in the community for recommendations about organizations or sites that would fit with your career aspirations. Taking the time to meet with faculty members to ask their opinion accomplishes two goals related to getting an internship interview. First, you will get to have a one-on-one conversation with the faculty member and he or she will learn more about you and how you plan to use the information they are teaching you in your career. Remember that faculty members usually love to talk about their specific areas and are flattered that you are getting something out of their classes. This interaction makes it more likely that the faculty member will feel confident in writing you a letter of recommendation for the internship or graduate school if they have gotten to know you better in an non-classroom context. Second, very often, faculty members in the Family Sciences are active in the community either as consultants, practitioners, board members, or via their research on community programs. Thus, they provide you with valuable insights into organizations that you could target for internships. An added bonus is when the faculty member can give you specific names of individuals integral in decision-making or are willing to personally recommend you to the organization.

There may also be people in your current network that you can access to help you find an internship interview, but might not immediately come to mind (See *Networking with less obvious internship sources*). These examples may also be shaped by the specific field you plan to enter, and by your decision about whether or not to stay in your college or university's town for your internship, move home, or move to a new location altogether. For example, if you plan to stay in your college town, then using the connections you may have made through your part-time job can be very useful; this way, you could let others know that you are planning an internship as well as tell them the type of work you are interested in doing. Even if you work in retail or you are a server at a restaurant, talking to coworkers, supervisors, and even regular customers can increase your network in the community. You never know who knows someone who might be helpful to you!

Networking with less obvious internship sources

Networking sources	Examples
Community roles	Part-time jobs Places you volunteer Mentorship programs
Non-academic organizations you belong to	Service organizations Church groups Community theater or other activities Part-time jobs
People you have the closest relationships with	Friends Family Roommates Friends' families Roommates families
People you know but not well	Dentist Hair Stylist Physician Former teachers, principals, guidance counselors Former coaches

The same logic can be applied to the two groups associated with people who know you, either well or just casually. Through putting the word out that you are actively looking for an internship and informing them of the type of environment you are interested in, people who are not directly related to your academic career may also turn out to be great sources for information on appropriate sites. As with faculty, you may even end up with a specific name of someone to contact at the organization. For example, think of the person who styles/cuts your hair. Imagine the number of people from all different jobs, careers, disciplines and environments that that person sees *on a weekly basis*. What an excellent way to increase your network contacts from one conversation with your hairstylist!

After identifying potential sources to approach, identify the person(s) within an organization you can contact for an interview. You should target the person most likely to supervise you. From strongest to weakest, most to least desirable, these individuals would hold positions such as: members of executive management (Executive Directors, Program Directors, Clinical Directors, etc); members of senior management (Human Resources, if it is a large organization); other supervisors or managers; other employees; and consultants doing business with an organization (DeLuca & DeLuca, 2001).

More importantly, how do you get these people to see you? One of the ways we help students make connections with people who are likely to interview them is by assigning them an Informational Interview. Students are required to select someone who works in an organization doing the type of work they are interested in pursuing and interview them about what they do, their professional development, educational background and so forth. By doing this activity, the student is building a relationship (it really is the key!) and is more likely to get an interview later. The student is still making connections within the organization even if the person who does the interview isn't the one who makes the decisions about internships. The Informational Interviewee can now make a personal recommendation of the student to the person who ultimately makes the decision.

In addition to Informational Interviews, we strongly encourage students to join professional organizations related to their field as student members. Fortunately for Family Science students, the National Council on Family Relations does allow student memberships for a nominal annual fee.

Even in professional organizations that do not allow undergraduate students to be members, it is possible to ask to be involved as a non-member. By joining or attending events as a non-member, you will have access to potential internships sites through conferences, meetings, workshops and so forth, which will further build your network *and* demonstrate your commitment to your field through your active involvement.

Similarly, becoming active in your community through volunteerism, activism, and engaging in groups or activities that interest you builds your network and your potential exposure to internship sites. Notice we are focused on community engagement, meaning the community in which you live in or plan to live in, not the university or college community. First, your internship is not likely to be on campus, and therefore you should be building your connections with your community at large. In addition, many university towns have a Town and Gown division where the university community is insulated from the community in general. While this is not always the case, it occurs often enough to have a moniker!

Lastly, we pay particular attention throughout this text to the role technology and virtual connections play in your professional identity, networking, and professional development. We understand that our audience (the Millennial generation) is socialized to text-based communication such as email, social networking sites, texting etc. Therefore, when looking for interviews for an internship, the question remains: 'to e or not to e!' There is significant utility in using emails versus mailed resumes, and social networking via LinkedIn versus attending meetings in person. We strongly advise you to make sure you are getting face-time with your network and not relying only on Internet or web-based methods of networking. Building your relationships (there is that word again) in person is essential to your successful marketing of yourself and your skills, because as an intern, you are an unknown entity. Those in decision-making capacities in the organizations where you would like to intern are more likely to hire you (a.k.a. take a risk) if they feel as though they have had some face-time and know who you are, rather than having to rely on your email or an Internet search of your name.

We recommend all of these activities because of their network-building utility and to encourage you to think outside the box when looking for internship sites and planning interviews. Through using these means, your contacts with potential interviewers don't have to be formal interview situations, but if your internship application materials come across their desk or you personally contact them regarding an interview with their organization, then they will know your face which will provide you with a distinct advantage.

SELF-ASSESSMENT

Now that you've identified ways to find out about organizations as well potential targets for requesting an interview, you need to start preparing for your interview. Before interviewing with a specific organization, begin to think about how you are going to market your abilities and potential during your interview. Start by making a list of the reasons why someone might hire you. You should be aiming to prove that you would add value to their organization; however, sometimes you are just in the right place at the right time. For example, I (Gonyea) have a good friend who is a restaurateur and if he experiences superb service while we are at a fine dining establishment, he attempts to recruit the person to work in his restaurants. While this may not be a Family Science example, it definitely illustrates that by doing what you do well, you will be constantly marketing yourself for other opportunities.

As you think about the reasons someone would hire you as in intern, think less in terms of why they would want to interview you and more in terms of what you can do for them or their organization. Complete the sentence, "I would add value to their organization by..." If you can't finish the sentence or can't come up with any of the ways you would add value to organizations that are doing work you aspire to do, you need to do more research or homework or you will struggle during the interview process.

We strongly recommend you complete the exercises in the Applying Your Knowledge at the end of this chapter in order to fully answer the questions you are likely to be asked during an interview. Again, the interview is your opportunity to sell your skills and potential value to an internship site. Be prepared with specific examples of your accomplishments and achievements outside of the classroom. Employers and internship supervisors aren't concerned about your grades on content, but rather how well you are able to use the content in real-world situations. For example, if you earned an A in your Adolescent Development course, how can you use that information in an adolescent relationship education program with teens at risk for early sexual behavior, teen pregnancy, or domestic violence? Similarly, how do your personality characteristics assist you in the tasks that you would be assigned to do? For example, how does your ability to successfully multitask the roles of being a student and a collegiate athlete simultaneously assist you in being able to manage deadlines during your internship working with migrant workers and their families? We encourage you to think beyond, "I have a passion for working with kids." While enthusiasm and passion are important and help you stay motivated to do the tasks assigned to you, they aren't selling points to a supervisor. Be specific about how your personal characteristics could translate into value for the organization or program where you want to intern.

Preparing for Your Interview

It may seem as though you've already put effort into the preparation for your interview. Really what you've been doing is gathering information you already know, about your favorite subject (you!), to prove your value to an organization and perhaps to yourself. Once you have scheduled an interview with a specific company, whether it is formal or informal, you should start your preparations for *that* interview by doing your research, rehearsing, and relaxing (DeLuca & DeLuca, 2001; Kador, 2002).

Research

The first step in prepping for an interview is researching the particular organization where you will be interviewing. You may have already thought through what you want and what you need from your internship. Review the Agency Research assignment you completed in Chapter 4 to be prepared for your interview.

Knowing this information will help you with think ahead to how you can help the organization accomplish its mission, goals, and programming (see 'Applying your Skills...Assessment').

Other information you will want to gather include the dress code, their use of technology, funding sources, reputation, and morale of the employees. What other agencies, organizations, or community groups do they interact with? What are the relationships between these groups? Have they had interns before and what was their experience like? Did they get the number of hours needed and were they able to have the experiences they planned for? Is the equipment you need provided for you (computer, tablet, etc) or will you need to use your own? This information will assist you in making a decision about whether this particular organization is a good fit for your internship goals (See Chapter 4).

We can hear you wondering, 'How do I find all of that out?' Simple, the way we learn anything now—Google it! Most of the information you are looking for about the company itself is available on the Internet. Use your technological savvy and put it to work for you. Start with the company's website which should have the mission statement, programs offered, a directory of employees, and perhaps even links to news items about community involvement, awards, or other recognition for the work they do. Your next step is to look up the key players in the organization with whom you will be working or who heads the programs in which you are most interested in contributing. You can see what their digital identity is, how well they have kept their personal and professional lives separate online, which will tell you a great deal about the technological culture of the organization. In fact, this may be one of the ways you can contribute to the organization if you find they need some help, or use this information in deciding whether or not you want the internship when it is offered to you later. Another method for looking up key players is through their LinkedIn profiles. Who are they connected to, how do they describe what they do and what they are interested in doing?

Researching the organization where you will interview accomplishes several goals. First, and most importantly, you will make a positive impression if you demonstrate your motivation, dedication, and initiative through finding out all the basic information before the interview. Second, you will have a basic outline of the company before the interview and can use your face-to-face time with the interviewer to fill in the blanks. And lastly, you will then be able to put together your skills, experiences, goals, and personal characteristics with what you know about the organization to really understand the value you add as an intern and communicate this during the interview.

The last part of doing your homework before the interview is making sure you have gathered any information they are likely to request, such as getting your references together. Make sure you have current contact information for your references and have asked them to be your references. Be aware of what types of information the interviewer may ask of them such as their relationship to you, how long they have known you, your job title and job description when they knew you. Provide this information to your references ahead of time so that they are not burdened with gathering this data or running the risk of appearing hesitant when contacted because they are trying to remember details. Lastly, consider that your references are likely to be asked about your overall performance and your ability to work as a team. For example, you ask a professor to be a reference because the course content is most related to your internship duties and you earned a high grade for the course, but you were also habitually late to class and with assignments, or didn't regularly show up for class at all. This professor is far more likely to either refuse to be a reference or he or she may discuss the negatives of your work habits versus the grade that you earned when contacted.

Rehearse

After doing the research about the company, your next step is to rehearse responses to likely questions. We recommend reviewing the list of the most commonly asked interview questions in DeLuca and DeLuca's (2001) book, *More Best Answers to the 201 Most Frequently Asked Interview Questions* to determine which interview questions would most likely be asked of you during an internship interview. Think through your responses, making sure to give concrete, specific examples that reference the evidence of your skills. Write out your responses to the questions, but don't stop there. It isn't enough to write out the response, you have to practice them out loud and in front of others. First, if you memorize your written responses, they end up sounding rehearsed. While we do want you to rehearse your answers, we don't want you to *sound* rehearsed because you will look less genuine, which will lead interviewers to judge you as less trustworthy. Also, you are more likely to get tripped up during the interview and less likely to recover if you have only memorized your answers. So, how do you rehearse but not sound rehearsed? See the Applying Your Knowledge section for a suggested solution to this dilemma!

Relax

The final step in your preparation for the interview is to relax. For some of you this seems like a crazy or impossible idea. However, you are much more likely to do well during your interview if you stay relaxed and take care of yourself before interviewing. As with an exam or presentation for class, getting a good night's sleep before the interview will greatly improve your chances of staying calm during the interview itself. As faculty members, we know this is easier to recommend than to do. Trust us, we walk into the classroom on an exam day and feel the tension and anxiety in the room like a highly humid day. If we can feel it, so can an interviewer, so make sure you practice relaxing.

One method for relaxing is to practice deep breathing. This is a great way to stay relaxed and to make sure that your brain has enough oxygen to think clearly, so it's a double win! Mind you, we don't mean do deep yoga breathing or heavy breathing: practice taking breaths that fill your lungs without making noises or sighing. Pay attention to keeping your shoulders pressed down, making it easier to draw a deep breath and appearing relaxed. A quick tip: if you breathe out longer than you breathe in, your brain thinks you are getting ready to sleep and will start relaxing the rest of your body.

Another suggestion for staying relaxed during an interview is to slow it down. Slower breaths, slower speaking, and thoughtful pauses will serve to keep your pace from reflecting anxiety. We tend to speed up our speech patterns when anxious or nervous, so paying attention to this will keep you going at a more relaxed pace.

Lastly, you know this topic—you! The interviewer is not trying to trick you or quiz you about what you know or can do. They are genuinely interested in learning about you and how you will fit in their organization. If you have done all the preparation that we have outlined in this section, you are completely ready to talk about how you can benefit their company, your goals for your internship, and how your experiences thus far make you a great intern candidate.

THE INTERVIEW ITSELF

An interview is your opportunity to demonstrate that you live up to what they have already decided they liked in your previous interactions, whether they be emails, phone calls, informational interviews, resumes, or official application materials. They already liked what they saw and your job is to reinforce these positive opinions of you and convey how credible and trustworthy you are. If you don't think you are right for the job, how is the interviewer supposed to think so?

We know of at least one instance of overselling that ended up damaging the credibility of the interviewee for an entry-level position with a graphic artist. The graphic artist was describing the compensation, the path toward advancement, and being realistic about the job description during the interview. He was describing the grunt work type tasks associated with the position until the new hire had proven their skill set on the job. The interviewee responded with an effusive, and we quote, "Oh, that's ok! I love menial tasks!" Needless to say, the interviewer was left with the impression of the interviewee being either desperate for a job or a liar. That is not the impression you want to leave!

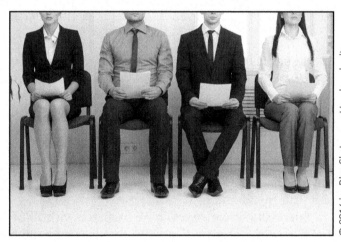

A similar mistake is to oversell your capabilities. You are interviewing for an internship, and you are expected to need supervision and guidance because you *are an intern* whose whole purpose in being there is to learn about the field and gain some experience. The interviewer will consider you unrealistic if you promote an attitude of knowing everything you need to know already, in which case, why bother with the internship, right? A better option is to acknowledge your goals for the internship, while also highlighting your ability to find the answers you need, develop relationships with those who can teach you, or your initiative.

One of our pet peeves during presentations in class is the use of verbal fillers. While this is addressed in Chapter 5 in self-presentation skills, it is worthy of repetition. Verbal fillers are those little verbal quirks used to fill empty spaces in a conversation or to transition to a new topic. They might be used when you are trying to think of an answer. Everyone has a personal favorite, but the most common are um, like, and uh. Avoid using these at all costs during your interview because they make you sound less intelligent that you are, less confident, and more immature.

Lastly, don't use obscure or convoluted verbiage when discussing the relative merits of your association with the esteemed organization. In other words, make sure that you sound like yourself. When you attempt to use jargon or over-complicated words, others interpret this as a lack of confidence (hiding behind jargon to hide a lack of depth or specificity), arrogance, or lack of genuineness. Keep in mind that use of language that reflects an understanding of the content, program, or other relevant material does sound impressive and demonstrate that you've done your homework; however, you should make sure that you incorporate this language in a way that you still sound like who you are. After all, they are interested in selecting *you* as an intern.

Qualities of successful interviewees.

- On time
- Neat and appropriately attired
- Has done the research on the organization
- Knows what (s)he has to offer and backs up claims with examples
- Enthusiastic
- Open (See chapter 5 for behaviors that convey openness)
- Credible
- Understands the organization's needs and goals

(Adapted from DeLuca & DeLuca, 2001)

© 2016 by Andrey_Popv. Used under license from Shutterstock, Inc.

Significant attention has been given to what **not** to do during an interview. The *Qualities of successful interviews* box lists the qualities of successful interviewees and provides examples of what you should concentrate on conveying during an interview. However, there are other considerations, such as when your interview is scheduled—this can actually have an impact on your chances. For example, try to avoid being the first person interviewed if you are in a pool of candidates. Interviewers haven't had a chance to refine how they are doing the interview and what they need to ask, so you end up being the guinea pig. Similarly, if at all possible, avoid scheduling interviews on Monday mornings or late on Fridays for obvious reasons. Neither of these time periods is conducive to having the interviewer focused on you and your qualifications.

Successful interviewees arrive prepared with all of the information they might be asked to provide. For example, bring fresh copies of your resume highlighting your skills and any relevant experiences the interviewer might want to know about. These are a great source of interview questions and you can easily discuss how these are related to the internship because you will have practiced those answers. Make sure that you have names and current contact information, such as phone numbers, emails, and addresses, for all of your references with you during your interview. Your goal is to make it as easy as possible for the interviewer to find out what they need to know to select you.

Presenting yourself well, also covered in more depth in Chapter 5, includes appearing and interacting with the interviewer as though you already have the internship. For example, dress as if you already work there, or perhaps even a little bit better. Interview clothes are usually one step up from what you would usually wear to work.   In addition, you should show sincere interest in the interviewer by using his or her name. Be calm and speak clearly when you relate positive stories about your experiences that reflect how well you would fit with their organization. Notice we said *positive* experiences. While interviewing, it is always best to focus on what you learned or how you grew from the experiences that led you to this moment. A big mistake is to focus on how those experiences didn't play out the way you thought they would or on how your supervisors were unfair—even if this is the case. In this instance, you should plan to discuss the positives from any experiences that you are likely to be asked about. For example, if you had a supervisor who didn't provide clear direction, you can frame that as having had the opportunity to learn how to evaluate immediate needs and prioritize tasks. Lastly, make sure that you ask questions about the organization to fill in the information you weren't able to gather before the interview. By doing so, you are demonstrating to the interviewer that you did your homework on their organization and are motivated. Also, ask questions about the internship itself, your duties, their expectations, if they have ever had interns before, what the qualities of a successful intern are, and where and what are their former interns doing now. Again, these are information for you, and also demonstrate to the interviewer that you are committed to getting the most out of the internship experience.

Some inexperienced interviewees miss the cues that the interview is coming to a close. Pay close attention to the nonverbal cues that say your interview is over. Some of these include body language of the interviewer. If the interviewer is looking at the clock, it probably means they have another interviewee coming in and need to stay on time. Other more obvious cues are when the interviewer stands up, sits up straight, opens the door, and other methods of nonverbally telling you that they need to close the interview. Usually these nonverbal cues have been preceded by questions such as, "Is there anything else you wish to discuss?" or "Do you have any remaining questions for us?" If you still have questions, ask how much time they have and prioritize the questions you have remaining. If you are short on time, ask if you can email the remaining questions to the interviewer. By doing so, you are winning points for being detail-oriented and having done your homework, but also for respecting their time and schedule.

Lastly, some of our students in more informal interview situations have been surprised by being asked, "So, do you want the internship?" at the conclusion of their interview. By preparing the way we've advised in this chapter, you should have all of the information you need to answer this question by the end of the interview. However, if you feel put on the spot for an answer and aren't quite sure, or you have two other places left to interview with, don't hesitate to ask for time to consider the offer, but always give a time frame for when you will provide the answer; "I am really excited about this opportunity to work with you. Let me review some of the information I've gathered today and call/email you on Monday with an answer." Responses such as this are appropriate any time, but particularly if the internship involves a commute, moving, or other logistical considerations. Be prepared for the question by evaluating the information you are gathering during the interview process so you will be ready in case the question is asked of you.

Tips for successful Skype or video call interviews

Skype or video call interviews are still an interview, therefore you should use all of the information about a traditional in-person interview while being aware of the unique challenges to these types of interactions. Suggestions for making the most of an interview using video technologies include:

- Keep distractions to a minimum
- Make sure you have reliable hardware and connection
- Test drive your set-up well before the interview. Set up your computer in the space you plan to use. Check the lighting, volume, and external noises. For example, as I (Gonyea) sit and write this chapter the windows are open and a dog is barking in the background— not good if I am on an interview.
- Make sure you have access to the space you plan to use for the interview during the interview time.
- Test drive your hardware including the sound quality.
- Make sure you look into the camera rather than where the faces are on your screen. Keep in mind that the interviewer is looking at either a larger monitor or projection screen.
- Also, remember they are judging your credibility and the best way to convey this is with direct eye contact.

Obvious Don'ts.

- Don't smoke, chew gum, or drink
- Don't bring friends or relatives. We have had several conversations with colleagues recently about interviewees for graduate programs bringing their mothers into their interview. The students didn't get into the program.
- Don't whine
- Don't focus on how the internship will benefit you.
- Don't look at your watch
- Don't be a one man/woman band add some 'we's'
- Don't forget to be yourself
- Don't forget to thank the interviewer for their time
- Don't forget to ask what and when the next step will be

AFTER THE INTERVIEW

You should go into your interview believing you are the best candidate. However, after the interview you should debrief yourself about how the interview went. Think about where you could have answered more completely or more succinctly; what other information could you have added to illustrate your points? What were the interviewers' reactions to what you said? Were they as you'd anticipated? Were the questions you prepared to answer asked of you and if not, how can you prepare more thoroughly for the next interview? Spend some time thinking about how to improve your performance during an interview. You can use this information after you graduate when you are interviewing for paid positions.

You also have the opportunity to make an impression on your interviewer by following up. It is standard to follow up with the interviewer by sending a thank you note either in writing or by email. In your thank you note, express your continued interest in the internship based on specific information you learned during the interview process. You can also specifically reference something about your interactions with the interviewer, letting him or her know you were paying attention. A thank you email is appropriate the day after your interview; however, if you are sending a snail mail thank you note, you should mail it directly after your interview so that the person receives it in approximately 2–3 days.

The follow-up serves two purposes after your interview. First, it gives you the opportunity for the interviewer to remember his or her interactions with you, particularly if you are in a pool of internship candidates. Second, it demonstrates that you understand the skills needed to act professionally and inspires confidence that you will represent the organization well if they were to select you.

APPLYING YOUR KNOWLEDGE

This chapter has provided you with a wealth of information on successful interviewing. Now, you have the opportunity to practice your interview skills using the knowledge that you've gained. Even if it is not required of your program or this course, schedule an Informational Interview with a professional in the field in which you want to work or intern. In this instance, you are the interviewer, but the experience gives you the chance to practice how you discuss your interest in the field. We've provided a set of sample questions you can use on page.

Another way to practice your interview skills is to complete a simulated interview with your university's career services office. Some universities offer simulated interviews online or you can schedule a mock interview with one of their staff members. If your university doesn't have these types of services or you think it would be best to interview with someone who knows your field better, you can ask a faculty member to pseudo interview you. For example, students who are preparing for graduate school interviews often ask us to mock interview them because we know what questions are likely to be asked about our respective areas of expertise.

INTERVIEW PREPARATION SELF-ASSESSMENTS

1 - Skills Assessment

Create a table listing at least 10 verbs associated with skills you possess in one column and evidence that proves you have that skill in a second column.

What Can I Do?	
Skill	**Evidence**
Apply developmental knowledge in community settings	*Generated a handbook for undergraduate students who are graduation mentors for adolescents attending an alternative high school*
1.	
2.	
3.	
4.	
5.	
6.	
7.	
8.	
9.	
10.	
11.	

(Adapted from DeLuca & DeLuca, 2001)

2 - Knowledge Assessment

Now, create a table listing at least 5 content areas in which you have expertise and evidence that proves you have that knowledge.

What Do I Know?	
Content	**Evidence**
Child Development	*Piaget's and Erickson's stages of development*
1.	
2.	
3.	
4.	
5.	

(Adapted from DeLuca & DeLuca, 2001)

3 - Personal Qualities Assessment

Next, list at least 5 adjectives that describe your personality and characteristics. Provide an example of *how* you demonstrate this quality in an Evidence column. For example:

What am I Like?	
Content	**Evidence**
Organized	*Developed binders for class content organized by chapter for each course taken*
1.	
2.	
3.	
4.	
5.	

(Adapted from DeLuca & DeLuca, 2001)

4 - Achievements

Next, list at least 5 of your achievements. Make sure you enter details about the achievement and how these are related to your role as an intern in the organization. For example:

Achievements		
Achievement	**Details (where, when, how much)**	**Applied to Internship**
Outstanding Undergraduate Research Poster	*Presented the design for an afterschool program I developed that incorporates physical activity into homework.* *Goal of the program: increase physical activity to reduce childhood obesity while increasing educational outcomes for high risk populations*	*I can implement the program in the YMCA afterschool program (internship site).* *Potential Internship Project related: evaluate the program using participant's BMI and homework grades*
1.		
2.		
3.		
4.		
5.		

(Adapted from DeLuca & DeLuca, 2001)

Name: Section: Date:

5 - Professional Development Plan

Lastly, list at least 5 areas, skills, or experiences you *would like* to have in order to grow professionally during your internship and in the early years of your career. Include your plan for acquiring the skills and experiences needed during your internship. For example:

Professional Development	
Skills & Experiences needed	**Plan during Internship**
Presentation skills	a) *Lead workshops for parents* b) *Present the results of the evaluation of the afterschool program to faculty (end of semester), the Board of Directors (during internship), and potential funders (after Internship)*
1.	
2.	
3.	
4.	
5.	

(Adapted from DeLuca & DeLuca, 2001)

Applying your Skills, Knowledge, and Achievements

Now that you have listed your skills, knowledge, and achievements, and assessed the ways these benefit your internship site and contribute to your professional development, it is time to prepare yourself to sell these to your internship site as reasons they should invest their time, energy, and resources into providing you with an internship. Using the table below, connect your skills, knowledge and achievements to your role as an *intern with a specific internship site*. Complete a chart like the one below for each internship you are interested in pursuing and either review prior to or bring this to your interview.

Organization needs: The ways my skills/experiences/internship role fill(s) this need?
Organization needs: The ways my skills/experiences/internship role fill(s) this need?
Organization needs: The ways my skills/experiences/internship role fill(s) this need?
Organization needs: The ways my skills/experiences/internship role fill(s) this need?
Organization needs: The ways my skills/experiences/internship role fill(s) this need?

(Adapted from DeLuca & DeLuca, 2001)

INFORMATIONAL INTERVIEW QUESTIONS

Before beginning your informational interview, you should note the name, title, company or organization the person works for, and the date. Next, you can ask questions like the ones we've supplied below.

1. How long have you worked for the organization?
2. What is your official title here?
3. Can you describe your primary duties?
4. What is the primary mission of the organization?
5. What are the requirements (educational, experience, etc.) for the position you hold?
6. What advancement opportunities are there for someone in your position?
7. What are the positives and negatives of your position?
8. What advice would you offer someone entering this field?
9. How do you maintains a balance between career and family?
10. Could you describe an ethical situation you've encountered in this position or in your career? What steps did you take to resolve the situation? What were the results of your decision?
11. Could I have brochures, literature, or publicity about the organizations' services and products?
12. Is there anything else I should know or ask about if I am interested in a career in this field?

AGENDAS

In this chapter, you read about four potential agendas during an interview: your agenda, your *hidden* agenda, the interviewers agenda, the interviewers *hidden* agenda. We can safely assume the interviewers agenda is to find out your qualifications, the degree of fit between you and the organization, and whether or they can meet the requirements for your institution (number of hours, type of project, level of oversight, etc.). Use this page to think through your own agendas and how you will accomplish them.

Your Agenda

List at least four items on your agenda for your interview and how you can accomplish that item. Make sure you list potential questions you can ask to be prepared when they ask you if you have any questions.

Your agenda items	Ways to accomplish your agenda
1.	
2.	
3.	
4.	
5.	

Your Hidden Agenda

Now, list at least four items on your *hidden* agenda and how you can accomplish that item. This is a bit trickier because you generally can't find out the information by asking a direct question. So, what do you want to find out without letting your interviewer know you want to find it out?

Your hidden agenda items	Ways to accomplish your hidden agenda
1.	
2.	
3.	
4.	
5.	

REFERENCES

DeLuca, M.J. & DeLuca, N.F. (1999). *Get a Job in 30 Days or Less*. New York: McGraw-Hill.

DeLuca, M. J. & DeLuca, N.F. (2001). *More Best Answers to the 201 Most Frequently Asked Interview Questions*. New York: McGraw-Hill.

Kador, J. (2002). *201 Best Questions to Ask on Your Interview*. New York: McGraw-Hill.

Thinking and Acting Ethically

OBJECTIVES:

➤ Summarize the importance of ethical education in the Family Sciences
➤ Identify the ethical principles, code, or standards associated with your internship or internship site
➤ Discriminate between absolutism and relativism with regard to ethics
➤ Explain the four categories of the Ethical Principles adopted by National Council on Family Relations (NCFR)
➤ Create an appropriate plan of action for ethical situations using the Minnesota Council on Family Relations (MCFR) Case Study Process provided in this chapter
➤ Analyze ethical dilemmas associated with your role as an intern

Imagine you are interning at a local sexual assault center and one of your chief responsibilities is working the rape crisis hotline. During your weekend shift, a young woman calls to report an acquaintance rape, telling you that while she was hanging out with mutual friends, she was sexually assaulted. She reports losing consciousness, having a gap of several hours that were unaccounted for, that she had not yet showered and was asking for help in how to proceed. In the course of telling you her account, she mentions the name of her assailant and you realize that he is the same person with whom your roommate has been flirtexting for the past couple of weeks. How do you approach the situation and which ethical or moral obligation is prioritized?

For some of you, the answer seems simple—the moral obligation to prevent harm (prevent future sexual assaults) outweighs all else. However, there are both ethical and legal ramifications to breaching confidentiality, not the least of which is damaging the potential criminal case resulting from this woman's report of sexual assault. You might feel this is an extreme circumstance or that it will not apply to you because you plan to work with a different population. Unfortunately, the situation outlined above is loosely based on a real event, and in our experience, each semester we have coordinated or supervised internships that have had similarly complex situations, regardless of the population or environments in which the students intern.

ETHICS EDUCATION

Given the emphasis on ethics education from national Family Science professional organizations and our own experiences with interns over the years, we feel that thorough coverage of ethical decision making, as part of a Family Science internship, is crucial for professional development. Not only does this better prepare students for their applied experiences, it heads off potentially damaging situations for community members, the organization, and the student intern.

In order to provide empirical evidence for the need to train such individuals to think and behave ethically, Knaub and Merdith (1991) surveyed Family Science practitioners about their ethics training. Their results indicate that the overwhelming majority of their participants had experienced an ethical dilemma in their career (Knaub & Merdith, 1991). The sheer proportion of those who reported encountering an ethical dilemma strongly suggests that you will too, whether either in your internship or your career. Of those who experienced an ethical dilemma, less than half had been taught how to handle such situations in their degree programs (Knaub & Meredith, 1991). Other results from the study indicate that those trained as clinicians (couple and family therapists) feel their training helped them to resolve the ethical dilemmas encountered in their careers, while those in non-clinical Family Science careers felt ill-equipped to handle ethical questions. Those that didn't have any exposure to ethical education felt that such training would have been helpful in managing the ethical situations they had encountered. Nearly all of those who participated in the study felt that Family Life educators should have a code of ethics (Knaub & Meredith, 1991). All of these data, taken together, provided the justification for the development of the ethical principles adopted by NCFR.

Adams and her colleagues (2001) outline the process by which NCFR used Knaub and Meredith's (1991) results to establish their ethical guidelines and principles and provide an overview of why new family scientists should be trained in ethical decision making. The authors suggest consideration of four pedagogical issues, two of which we attempt to address in our coverage of ethical decision making in this chapter. Here, we provide a starting point for students to think critically about ethics through presenting the *Ethical Principles and Guidelines for Family Scientists* (MCFR, 2009) and provide an overview of the ethical approaches utilized by NCFR. Additionally, we offer opportunities to practice ethical decision making skills through the case studies found in the Application of Knowledge section.

ETHICAL DECISION MAKING MODELS

The old adage, 'a failure to make a decision, is a choice in itself,' summarizes a common approach to ethical situations. Unfortunately, any failure to make an informed decision or take an action, results in *deciding by default* (Kirsch, 2009). In other words, by not deciding on a course of action you are deciding to let the default action occur. This *deciding by default* is accompanied by a different set of ethical considerations; therefore professionals are expected to engage in ethical decision making at a higher level (Kirsch, 2009).

Multiple models of ethical decision making for professionals exist in the literature due to the higher demand and the specific challenges faced by the discipline on the essential tasks, roles, and responsibilities of the field. Most ethical decision making models follow the same basic formula seen in Figure 7.1, adding information or ethical imperatives specific to that discipline. This text reviews two models relevant to Family Science with particular emphasis on and application of those adopted by NCFR.

Realm-Individual Process-Situation [RIPS] model

The Realm-Individual Process-Situation (RIPS; Swisher, Arslanian, & Davis, 2005) model of ethical decision making uses the basics of decision making as outlined in the previous section and adds specific processes to resolve ethical situations. The RIPS model is outlined in Table 7.1.

FIGURE 7.1. Basic Ethical Decision Making Steps

1) Identify the ethical issue or problem in the situation
2) Identify the relevant ethical standard or principle
3) Identify the potential courses of action and their consequences
4) Decide upon an action
5) Evaluate the results of the action

TABLE 7.1. Realm-Individual Process-Situation Model

1) Recognize and Define the Ethical Issue	
2) Reflect on:	Relevant facts and contexts
	Stakeholders
	Consequences
	Laws, duties, obligations, and ethical principles
	Professional Resources
	Tests for right vs. wrong
Decide on the right thing to do following:	Rules-based approach
	Ends-based approach
	Care-based approach
Implement, evaluate, and reassess	

(Swisher, Arslanian, & Davis, 2005)

Recognizing and Defining the Ethical Issue. In Step 1, the ethical situation is evaluated in terms of the Realm, Individual Process, and Situation before moving on to Step 2. The Realm refers to the domain of life in which the ethical situation falls: Individual, Organizational/Institutional, or Societal (Swisher, Arslanian, & Davis, 2005). The issues that confront individuals and families can overlap realms; however, the specific ethical situation being faced is likely to be confined to one of these. For example, in the example given at the start of this chapter, the intern's dilemma about the alleged assailant would fit within an Organizational/Institutional domain due to the formal policies about confidentiality and the legal issues in place governing the ethical issue at hand.

The Individual Process portion of the RIPS model requires an analysis of the situation facing the relevant parties in terms of: moral sensitivity; moral judgment; moral motivation; moral courage/ego strength; and moral failure (See Table 7.2; Swisher, Arslanian, & Davis, 2005). All of the elements in Individual Processes must be addressed at some point in the process of making an ethical decision; however, they do not need to be addressed in any particular order.

TABLE 7.2. Individual Processes

Individual Process	
Moral sensitivity	An awareness that an ethical issue exists
Moral judgment	Consideration of the potential courses of action and their potential consequences for all involved
Moral motivation	The force that compels you to consider the possible courses of action
Moral Courage/Ego strength	The strength to take action to correct a wrong
Moral Failure	A failure to have any one of the other four components of Individual Processes

(Swisher, Arslanian, & Davis, 2005)

The remaining element in the definition of the ethical issue at hand is the Situation. In this component of the RIPS model, practitioners assess the type of ethical situation with which they are confronted. In particular, is it an ethical problem, distress, dilemma, temptation, or a silence? Ethical problems are situations that threaten a practitioner's moral duties or values. An ethical distress is when a practitioner knows the action she or he should take, but barriers to taking the action exist. An ethical dilemma exists when two or more correct courses of action exist and the practitioner is faced with a 'right vs. right' choice. An ethical temptation is when there is both an ethically correct and an ethically incorrect course of action, and the practitioner chooses the ethically incorrect action for some reason. Lastly, silence is when practitioners decide by default, as discussed earlier: they choose not to take any action, thereby letting the situation run its course with the concomitant consequences (Kirsch, 2009).

Deciding the right thing to do. As noted above, decisions about the course of action to be taken are further broken down in terms of the approach practitioners use to arrive at their decision. In a Rule-based approach, the decision would be made in strict accordance with ethical codes, standards, or guidelines in place for the profession. The use of a Rule-based approach can be quite challenging, even though this seems the safest approach and in keeping with the legal issues that may govern the situation. For instance, many professions related to Family Science have guidelines for ethical behavior, but these do not clearly specify the course of action to be taken related to various ethical situations.

The Ends-based approach is based in beneficence and non-malfeasance. In other words, those using the Ends-based approach make their decisions centered upon a desire to choose the action that results in the most good for the most people. The most good is balanced with the desire to do the least harm to the fewest people as well.

Lastly, those making decisions from a Care-based approach are those that decide on a course of action based on their own preference for how they would like to be treated in the same circumstances. This is an important perspective for two reasons. First, though the Care-based approach follows the golden rule of treating others as you want to be treated (Kirsch, 2009), there is limited consideration for the differences in experiences between the practitioner and the person whom the decision affects.

Notice that the RIPS model (Swisher, Arslanian, & Davis, 2005) provides a process for evaluating the situation rather than providing direct answers about what actions to take to resolve the situation. While this is a useful model for professionals with both experience and an established support network for consultation, interns will not yet have access to these essential components that aid ethical decision making. Therefore, students, interns, and new professionals require more direct guidance and training in appropriate ways to resolve ethical situations. Thus, we recommend an option that gives interns and new professionals more structure and guidance in the form of the NCFR 'relational ethics' approach.

NCFR Relational Ethics Approach

This text focuses on the ethical principles of NCFR as written by the Minnesota Council on Family Relations (MCFR; 2009) in an effort to provide more direct guidance to students and interns as they attempt to develop their ethical decision making skills. In addition, the NCFR ethical principles are inclusive of the wide variety of organizations, populations, and community issues that strive to improve lives and strengthen families. Despite the ethical principles' focus on Family Science, the approach and process adopted by NCFR can be applied to multiple disciplines' ethical standards and are useful guides of responsible, professional actions across a wide range of internships.

NCFR espouses using multiple approaches for thinking critically about ethics and ethical situations in order to appropriately address the multi-layered complexity of ethical decision making. For example, the ethical principles represent static ideas about the field, while humans and their relationships are necessarily complex and dynamic. Thus, an approach that solely addresses the principles will not reflect the considerable gray areas inherent in most ethical situations. Likewise, an ethics approach that only addresses relativity will provide little to no guidance for interns and new professionals. NCFR uses three perspectives in their approach to ethical decision making: relational ethics, principles approach, and virtues ethics (MCFR, 2009).

The *relational ethics approach* provides an umbrella under which the various Family Science professionals operate through the awareness that families and those who work with them are organized according to

FIGURE 7.2. Ethical decision making according to ethical principles adopted by NCFR

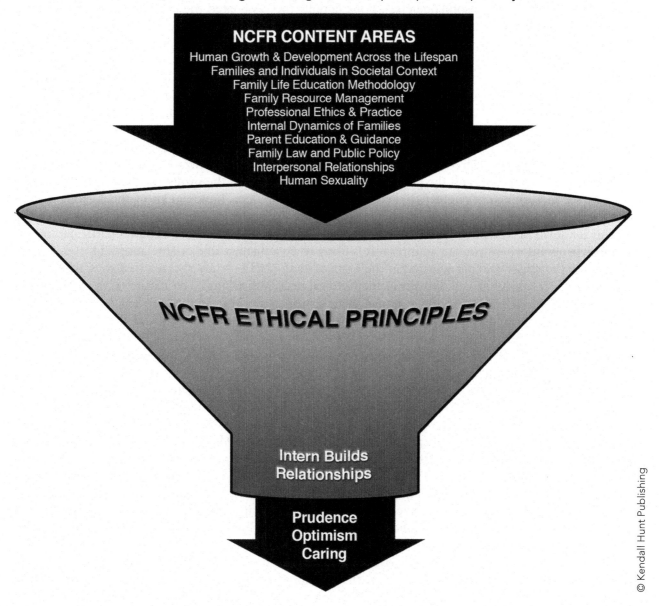

relationships with one another. From an internship perspective, these relationships are governed by the role the intern takes with the family (e.g. educator, interventionist, facilitator, etc.). In addition, the role is the method through which the intern builds a relationship with individuals and families and also through which the intern conveys the NCFR Content areas (NCFR, 2011) in Family Science work as outlined in Figure 7.2. The *ethical principles approach* then outlines the behaviors and priorities used in these 10 content areas. Lastly, attention to *virtues ethics* allows family scientists to acknowledge the values associated with working in areas affecting individuals' and families' lives. A virtues ethics approach has a two-tiered approach, the first being virtues for every profession, such as justice, and the second being those that are needed for ethical practice. In the case of the NCFR, this second level of ethical virtues include caring, prudence, and hope (NCFR, 2011).

In an effort to evaluate the processes by which family therapists working in small communities make ethical decisions about dual relationships, Gonyea, Wright, and Earl-Kulkosky (2014) surveyed family therapists who practice in rural counties, with particular emphasis on therapists who belong to minority populations. Participants reported that they were most likely to use their professional judgment as a basis for their ethical decision-making. The family therapists who participated in the study offered insight into how they used professional judgment or how they made the decision whether or not to recuse themselves (refer to someone else). For example, they evaluated the perceived need for services, the severity of the need, or their own expertise in a particular area (Gonyea, et al., 2014).

As established earlier, as interns you are still developing professional judgment, and therefore we strongly suggest that you rely on your supervisors' professional judgment and use that as a tool for learning how to make ethical decisions in the future. The exception to this would be when you are being asked to do something that seems inappropriate or wrong as in the examples in Chapter 5.

Participants indicated using their professional judgment in three specific domains: level of benefit or detriment, context, and nature of the relationship. While aware of the challenges of dual relationships, participants were more concerned with the degree of benefit to the clients. These results apply to internships with regard to the degree of benefit from participation in the organization or program, compared with the lack of benefit should the person/family not participate in the program.

The second domain of context applied to an internship reflects how you know the person. Participants in the Gonyea, et al., (2014) study reported sometimes engaging in dual relationships when the person is known professionally versus personally. For example, if your dentist's child is participating in a summer program where you are an intern, it is likely to be a manageable dual relationship.

Family therapists who participated in the Gonyea et al. (2014) study also referred to evaluating the nature of the relationship as a domain in their ethical decision making. The nature of the relationship denoted the level of intimacy in the potential dual relationship or the degree of interaction between the therapist and the potential client. For interns, this would translate to evaluating the likelihood of seeing this person working at a grocery store while you are shopping; there is a lesser degree of intimacy in this situation than someone with whom you socialize, with whom your family or spouse socializes, or if you share a specific activity such as an exercise class or a church choir.

The results of the Gonyea et al. study (2014) support the need for being well-informed about the ethical principles of your profession as well as having a well-developed and practiced process for arriving at an appropriate course of action when confronted with ethical situations. We recommend a thorough understanding of the MCFR ethical principles (See Appendix A; MCFR, 2009) since Family Science students engage in diverse specialties within the discipline. The MCFR (2009) ethical principles provide comprehensive guidelines for roles, behaviors, and virtues associated with all of the relationships students interning or working in Family Science might encounter across all populations and internship sites. The ethical principles are organized according to the roles in which Family Science interns engage: Relationships with Parents and Families; Relationships with Children and Youth; Relationships with Colleagues and the Profession; and Relationships with Community/Society.

Think back to Chapter 5 and the coverage of creating appropriate professional boundaries. What do you notice about the topics covered in that section and the organization of the MCFR (2009) ethical principles? Not surprisingly, they cover the same types of relationships (e.g. Chapter 4 boundaries between you and your peers and boundaries between you and those with whom you work). The preceding information refers to professional behaviors, but these behaviors are directly related to the ethical expectations about boundaries as put forth by NCFR. Think back to those specific examples in Chapter 5 (dual relationships, gifts, etc.) and consider the ethical implications given what you've learned in this chapter. Now, rather than thinking about how you will look in terms of your level of professionalism, you should be considering how your actions may be tied to ethical violations of your profession or upholding the virtues associated with your profession, such as caring, prudence, and hope. How does this change the way you think about those situations?

TECHNOLOGY AND ETHICS

Throughout the text, we have attempted to provide specific guidance related to interns' use of technology in its various forms. In part, this stems from an acknowledgment that Millennials, who have spent their entire lives surrounded by information technologies in the form of tablets and smartphones, represent the first generation to enter the workforce. Millennials, your generation, may encounter ethical situations and dilemmas heretofore unseen by supervisors and are likely to have a very different experience, comfort with, and reliance upon the use of technology in professional settings than these supervisors. Therefore, we address the potential ethical issues associated with technology, specifically ethical decision making with regard to social networking sites [SNS].

Technologies such as the Internet and SNSs have distinct disadvantages for those who work with families. As discussed in Chapter 5, the use of technology for work or internships can lead to the blurring of boundaries between personal and professional lives. For those in Family Life Education or clinical work, particularly demanding in terms of emotional engagement, the indistinct boundaries can potentially lead to compassion fatigue (Negash & Sahin, 2011). However, the use of SNSs or other communication technologies lead to greater connectivity with peers, colleagues, and supervisors (Gonyea et al., 2014; Kellen, et al., 2015).

The need for appropriate boundaries, protecting confidentiality, and an awareness of the potential for decreased objectivity during your internship have been discussed previously and represent the three most obvious conflicts faced when using technologies (Kellen, et al., 2015; Zur, Williams, Levahot, & Knapp, 2009). According to their respective ethical guidelines set down by the Association for Marriage and Family Therapy (AAMFT, 2012) and the MCFR (2009) ethical principles, those working with families and individuals need to be aware of their responsibility to set appropriate boundaries with clients or constituent families as well as respect and maintain confidentiality. Though Kellen and her colleagues (2015) do not present a model of ethical decision making per se, they do offer a set of guiding questions family therapists, and by default family scientists, should ask themselves when confronted with potential SNS interactions. Their guiding questions can be found in Figure 7.3 where we have substituted the term *therapist* with *Family Science intern* or *intern*.

FIGURE 7.3. Guiding Questions for Social Networking Site use with clients and families

1. What is the reason for using the SNS? How does this influence your opinion about the appropriateness of using/contacting someone through an SNS?
2. How could contact on SNSs potentially impact clients, therapy and/or the family system?
3. How would connection through an SNS have the potential of developing multiple relationships, or how could the Family Science intern safeguard against developing multiple relationships?
4. What are some ways that confidentiality may be compromised or can be protected using SNS?
5. How is the client's/therapist's [or Family Science intern's] privacy impacted through different behaviors on SNSs (e.g., friending, searching for profiles, etc.)?
6. What responsibilities does the intern have, if any, when creating or using SNS accounts?
7. How would contact through an SNS impact an intern in a professional context?
8. How could contact through an SNS increase the liability of the therapist?

Additional considerations:
- How might your responses change depending upon the following client factors?
  - Age
  - Ethnicity
  - Gender
  - Sexual orientation
  - Current diagnosis
  - Therapeutic relationship
  - Role in the family
- How do your responses vary when an intern is connecting with a client, peer or a supervisor?
- How would your responses change depending on the context of your interaction (e.g., family, individual, etc)?
- What are appropriate ways the intern can communicate his or her decisions with clients?
- How does this situation present unique challenges to communicating through SNSs when compared with other means of communication?

(Adapted from Kellen et al., 2015)

APPLYING YOUR KNOWLEDGE

Students often find it relatively easy to sit in a classroom and decide upon the most appropriate, or ethical, decision in a given situation. However, when faced with these situations in person there is little time for analysis before needing to make some sort of response, often the 'official' response when you are interacting with community members. When faced with a potential ethical dilemma during your internship, we strongly suggest you take the time to consider the entire situation before responding. While this might seem awkward, your internship is the best opportunity to ask for time to reflect since you have the excuse of being a trainee or an intern!

In order to prepare you for those moments, we devote a significant portion of this chapter to providing you the opportunity to practice your ethical decision making skills using the process and ethical principles adopted by NCFR. As you work through the case studies, think about the information you are given and what additional information you would want or should consider as you think about the most appropriate course of action. To begin with, review the Ethical Principles for Parent and Family Life Educators in Appendix A (MCFR, 2009) that were discussed earlier in this chapter. Next, review the steps outlined in the Case Study Process at the end of this chapter (Appendix B; MCFR 2009) and use this process for each of the following vignettes.

Case Study 1

You are a female intern working with a group of adjudicated youths and their families in a community-based, first-offender diversion program. The adolescents, ranging in age from 14 to 18 years, participate in multiple family groups that are part didactic and part experiential, sometimes breaking into separate youth and parent groups. During these breakout sessions, you are responsible for facilitating the group process in the youth group. However, during these sessions, the mostly male adolescents are more focused on discussing what you are wearing, how you look, asking about your relationship status, and commenting on what plans you might have for the weekend.

Case Study 2

You are an intern with an adolescent relationship skills program through a local Extension service. One of the components in the course is a weekend trip to a ropes course at a state park. Throughout the course of the weekend, you participate with your group in various fun and exciting activities that build communication, negotiation, and collaboration skills. You Instagram your experiences throughout the weekend and the next week, several of the adolescents on your trip want to follow you on Instagram to have access to the pictures.

What other information do you need in order to use the case study process as outlined in Appendix B?

What other questions should you ask about this particular scenario in order to understand the ethical principles at work?

_____

_____

_____

_____

_____

_____

_____

_____

_____

_____

_____

_____

_____

_____

_____

_____

_____

_____

_____

_____

Case Study 3

You are working as an intern in a summer day camp for children with physical disabilities and you notice that a child in your program has begun to be more aggressive lately, often hitting other children, reacting very strongly to small or imagined offenses from other children. During the parent and family day at the camp, you have the opportunity to interact with the child's parent, who appears dismissive of your concerns and reports not seeing these behaviors at home. Approximately a week later, you notice bruises on the child's upper arms.

What other information do you need in order to use the case study process as outlined in Appendix B?

What other questions should you ask about this particular scenario in order to understand the ethical principles at work?

_____

_____

_____

_____

_____

_____

_____

_____

_____

_____

_____

_____

_____

_____

_____

_____

_____

_____

_____

Case Study 4

The parent of a child from your internship has been flirting with you for the first several weeks you are there. You are likewise attracted to the person but haven't responded with anything other than casual flirtation because you are aware of the boundaries necessary for interacting with those you work with through your internship. Today, the person made a move and asked for your number to text you and asked to friend/follow you on social media.

_____

_____

_____

_____

_____

_____

_____

_____

_____

_____

_____

_____

_____

_____

_____

_____

_____

_____

_____

Case Study 5

You are working as an intern serving refugee families in your community as a parent educator. One of the families with which you work has three children aged 3, 7, and 10. During a conversation with the 10 year-old child, the child reports that the family of five all sleep in one bed. The family shares an apartment with another unrelated family of five, who also share one bed in the second bedroom. All of the children (six total) are often left in the care of the eldest one, who happens to be the 10 year-old child with whom you are working.

_____

_____

_____

_____

_____

_____

_____

_____

_____

_____

_____

_____

_____

_____

_____

_____

_____

_____

_____

Appendix A

Ethical Principles for Parent and Family Life Educators

I. Relationships with Parents and Families

1. We will be aware of the impact we have on parents and family relations.
2. We will strive to understand families as complex, interactive systems where parents have the primary responsibility as educators, nurturers, and limit-setters for their children.
3. We will respect cultural beliefs, backgrounds, and differences and engage in practice that is sensitive to the diversity of child-rearing values and goals.
4. We will help parents and other family members recognize their strengths and work with them to set goals for themselves, their children, and others.
5. We will respect and accept parents and other family members for who they are, recognizing their developmental level and circumstances.
6. We will support and challenge parents to continue to grow and learn about parenting and their child's development.
7. We will communicate respectfully and clearly with all family members.
8. We will communicate openly and truthfully about the nature and extent of services provided.
9. We will support diverse family values by acknowledging and examining alternative parenting practices that support healthy family relationships.
10. We will include parents and other family members as partners in problem solving and decision-making related to program design and implementation.
11. We will be proactive in stating child guidance principles and discipline guidelines and encourage non-violent child rearing.
12. We will create data privacy and confidentiality guidelines respectful of family members and protective of their legal rights.
13. We will provide a program environment that is safe and nurturing to all family members.
14. We will ensure that all family members have access to and are encouraged to participate in family life education.
15. We will support family members as they make decisions about the use of resources to best meet family needs.
16. We will support healthy interpersonal relationships among all family members.
17. We will encourage parents and other family members to reflect upon their values regarding sexuality and promote the healthy sexual development and well being of each family member.

II. Relationships with Children and Youth

1. We will treat children and youth with respect and sensitivity to their needs and rights as developing persons.
2. We will strive to understand children and youth in the context of their families.
3. We will do no harm to children and youth and insist on the same from others.
4. We will advocate for children and youth and their best interests at the same time that we work with the parents and other family members.

From *Ethical Thinking and Practice for Parent and Family Life Educators* by Ada Alden, Dawn Cassidy, Betty Cooke, and Glen Palm. Copyright © 2009 by Minnesota Council on Family Relations, www.mcfr.net. Reprinted by permission.

5. We will provide environments that are respectful of children and youth and sensitive to their developmental and individual needs.
6. We will support the right of all children and youth to have access to quality education, health, and community resources.

III. Relationships with Colleagues and the Profession

1. We will value and promote diversity in staff.
2. We will provide staff with policies and support systems for addressing difficult situations with family members, colleagues, and others.
3. We will follow data privacy policies that meet legal standards and are based on respect for family members.
4. We will follow the mandatory reporting of abusive family behavior in a respectful and prudent manner.
5. We will define our role as parent and family life educators and practice within our level of competence.
6. We will recognize the difference between personal and professional values in our professional interactions.
7. We will support the ongoing development of a knowledge base that guides us towards ethical and effective practice.
8. We will be committed to ongoing professional development to enhance our knowledge and skills.

IV. Relationships with Community/Society

1. We will be knowledgeable about community resources and make and accept informed, appropriate referrals.
2. We will be aware of the boundaries of our practice and know when and how to use other community resources for the benefit of family members.
3. We will communicate clearly and cooperate with other programs and agencies in order to best meet family needs.
4. We will advocate for laws and policies that reflect our changing knowledge base and the best interests of parents, families, and communities.
5. We will respect and uphold laws and regulations that pertain to our practice as parent and family life educators and offer expertise to legal authorities based on professional knowledge.

Appendix B

Case Study Process

Introduction to Process

This process is provided as one concrete way for small groups of parent and family life educators to carefully examine an ethical dilemma using the approaches described earlier. It is critical to practice ethical thinking in this concrete manner to become familiar with both the principles and the process. This process can be done in approximately one hour as a part of staff meetings.

Process Steps

Steps 1 through 3 focus on ethical thinking. This is important; give it plenty of time. Practitioners tend to leap to brainstorming possible actions/solutions before thoroughly engaging in the process.

Step 1. Identification of Relationships: Identify important relationships in the situation using the educator role as the primary focal point.

   a. What is the relational field – what are all potential relationships in the case?
   b. What is the primary caring relationship the educator needs to address in this case? (Examples: educator to family member, educator to group, educator to another staff person)
   c. What do we know about this relationship – quality, stage of development, etc.?

Step 2. Identification of Principles: Look over the list of principles to identify those that apply to the important relationship(s) in this situation. Decide which principles may be relevant to guiding ethical behavior. Are there any additional principles that might apply? Which are the three or four most relevant principles? Why? (Spend some time alone to select principles before discussing in small group.)

Step 3. Identification of Contradictions/Tensions: What are some potential/actual contradictions or tensions among or between relevant principles?

Step 4. Identification of Possible Solutions: Brainstorm possible actions by the parent and family life educator – keeping in mind the relationship(s), the relevant principles, and the virtues.

Step 5. Selection of Actions: Select one action or combination of actions to use that reflects adherence to the ethical principles. All of the principles are important and should be addressed in a thoughtful and respectful manner.

REFERENCES

Adams, R.A., Dollahite, D.C., Gilbert, K.R., & Keim, R.E. (2001). The development and teaching of the Ethical Principles and Guidelines for Family Scientists. *Family Relations, 50,* 41–48.

American Association for Marriage and Family Therapy. (2012). AAMFT Code of Ethics. Retrieved from http://www.aamft.org/imis15/Documents/Final 2012 AAMFT Code of Ethics.pdf

Gonyea, J.L., Wright, D., & Earl-Kulkosky, T. (2014). Navigating dual relationshiops in rural communities. *Journal of Marital & Family Therapy, 40(1),* 125–136.

Kellen, K., Schoenherr, A.M., Turns, B., Madhusudan, M., & Hecker, L. (2015). Ethical decision-making: Potential ethical and clinical implications for marriage and family therapists. *The American Journal of Family Therapy, 43,* 67–83.

Kirsch, S. (2009). Ethical decision making: Application of a problem-solving model. *Topics in Geriatric Rehabilitation, 25(4),* 282–291.

Knaub, P.K. & Meredith, W. (1991). Ethical dliemmas experience by family scientists: Implications for ethics education. *Home Economics FORUM, 6* 14–19.

Minnesota Council on Family Relations. (2009). *Ethical Thinking and Practice for Family Life Educators.* Minneapolis, MN.

National Council on Family Relations. (2011). *Family Life Education Content Areas.* Minneapolis, MN.

Negash, S. & Sahin, S. (2011). Compassion fatigue in marriage and family therapy: Implications for therapists and clients. *Journal of Marital and Family Therapy, 37(1),* 1–13.

Swisher, L., Arslanian, L, & Davis, C., (2005). The Realm-Individual Process-Situation (RIPS) model of ethical decision making. *HPA Resource, 5(3),* 3–8.

Zur, O., Williams, M.H., Lehavot, K., & Knapp, S. (2009). Psychotherapist self-disclosure and transparency in the Internet age. *Professional Psychology: Research and Practice, 40(1),* 22–30. Doi:10.1037/a0014745

Making Strategic Connections

"Several requirements go into finding that first job. Boiling it down to bumper-sticker length, think; Networking, internships, grades" (Felson, 2001, p. 14).

OBJECTIVES

By the end of this chapter you should be able to:

➤ Describe the differences between types of networks and the function they play in your career development
➤ Identify the role of networking in your professional development
➤ Create a plan for evaluating the breadth and strength of your professional network
➤ Develop goals for building your professional network during your internship
➤ Articulate the relationships between network structure, social resources, network benefits, and organizational outcomes
➤ Differentiate between the ways women and men network and the utility of each method
➤ Develop appropriate strategies for online networking

IT ISN'T WHAT YOU KNOW OR WHO YOU KNOW...

It's Whom You Can Meet

Imagine for a moment that you have invented something amazing, something that will revolutionize the world as we know it. How would you have your invention turned into something marketable? To whom would you present your idea to prototype it? How would production of your invention be financed? Whether we are talking about an invention or your career, the relationships you build with others, starting during your internship, are likely to lead to your success. Your internship is the perfect time to build relationships with three key groups of people: those who possess more knowledge and experience than you; those who possess different types of knowledge; and those who already have connections to important people in your chosen field. This chapter will help you learn about the different types of networks and their importance to your career development, as well as help you develop networking goals for your internship. You will also evaluate your existing network and learn concrete strategies for building the network that will lead to achieving those goals.

Many students and new employees are under the impression that working *really hard* will lead to success, as measured in grades, income, or career advancement. While mastering content in your courses and a strong work ethic are incredibly valuable, it is equally important to demonstrate your mastery of content through field-based experiences to key professionals. In other words, networking during your internship is an essential component to finding employment and advancing within your career. Networking becomes paramount to your success in a highly competitive job market in which 58% of recent college graduates (ages 22–27) are currently working in jobs that do not require a college education (Abel, Dietz Su, 2014; See Table 8.1 *Current Trends in Employment Rates*).

TABLE 8.1. Current Trends in Employment Rates.

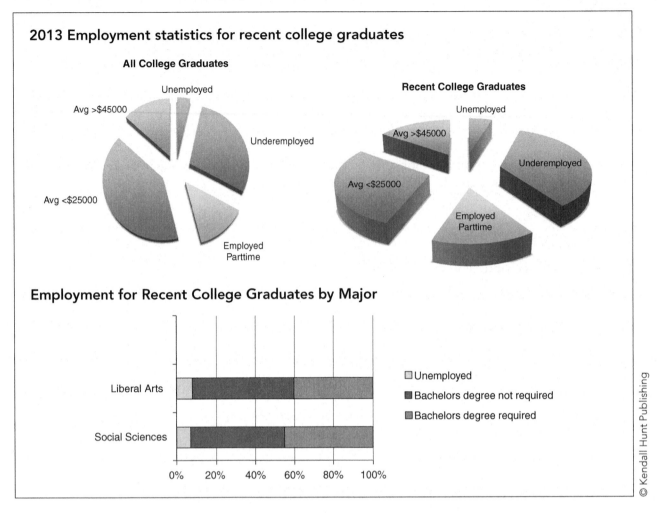

Your internship experience coupled with having a network of individuals who are trustworthy and familiar to potential employers will serve to offset the preconceived notions these employers may have of recent college graduates. For example, research indicates that 66% of those in hiring positions will overlook recent college graduates for an open position because they are believed to be unprepared for the workplace (Adecco Staffing, 2013). However, you have a greater likelihood of getting an interview when the person evaluating your application knows someone you worked with during your internship. Your ability to list respected sources as references, mention in your cover letter work you have done with the peers of potential employers', or even have your network members contact their peers about what a great job you have done, will counter the idea that you aren't prepared to be an employee.

Throughout this chapter you'll learn that the purpose of networking is to help you build your social capital during your internship. If you are indeed clear about your intentions to build connections and make plans to excel at networking, you are more likely to excel at your career (Garavan, Hogan, & O'Donnell, 2003).

TYPES OF NETWORKS

Before exploring models of social capital and gendered strategies for networking, it makes sense to identify the different types of networks that you currently have and those you need to develop related to your internship and your future career. You are likely to already have a well-developed *informal* network of groups of individuals who share your views and perhaps meet irregularly to discuss common interests. Many of these might be considered *community-based* networks that are broad-based groups such as churches or social organizations. The purpose of your internship is to develop your *formal* network of professional organizations that may require you to pay fees for which you will receive newsletters and be able to engage in networking activities related to your profession (Ehrich, 1994).

Within some of these broadly defined networks are those that are likely to be organized by function rather than by interest. For example, within informal, community-based, and formal networks, you may also engage in a *task* network. These networks enable the exchange of resources in order to accomplish project related tasks and might be found in professional organizations as well as church groups. *Friendship* networks might be found in the broader networks as well. Friendship or social networks are based on closeness and trust, a relationship quality rather than a function or a setting. Lastly, there is your *career* network, comprised of your relationships with supervisors, mentors, sponsors, and so forth that provide you with career advice and assist you with increasing your visibility within your organization, or from whom you can learn (Ibarra, 1995). As an intern, you are most likely in need of developing your formal, task-oriented, career networks such that you can increase the reach of your network and increase your employability.

IMPORTANCE OF BUILDING SOCIAL CAPITAL

The statistics in the introductory section of this chapter present a fairly clear picture about the need to distinguish yourself from your peers who are also entering the job market. One of the most certain ways to obtain a job offer is through an employee referral. In other words, you are more likely to get a job offer when you already know someone who works for that company; in fact, 80% of all available jobs aren't even posted in classifieds or on Internet job boards (Bradford, 2005). Strangely, this completely opposite to the ways recent college graduates think they *should* be searching for a job; 90% of those actively job searching think the only way to get their next job is to apply online. Yet 80% of those searching for jobs get their next job through someone they know (Feldstein, 2012) and 60% of people report that they found their last job through networking (Bradford, 2005).

The advantages of networking include building multiple developmental relationships (Wang, 2009) as well as information exchange, developing collaboration skills and professional alliances, acquiring new knowledge, increasing your visibility, and increasing your professional social support (Linehan & Scullion, 2008). Through these experiences and skills, you can develop a more diverse network that will extend your reach into different social circles. An extended reach results in enhanced career opportunities, which in turn makes it easier to find a job and results in faster promotion when you do find one (Baker, 2000; Ibarra, 1993).

These advantages are directly related to the development of both professional skills and networking skills that will lead to more opportunities, and therefore potentially more advancement, in your career. In an investigation of their impact on opportunities and advancement, Forret and Dougherty (2004) examined five specific groupings of networking behaviors: maintaining professional contacts, engaging in professional activities, participating in community activities, increasing internal visibility, and socializing outside of the workplace. Examples of behaviors in each of these categories are found in Table 8.2 *Types of Networking Behaviors*.

The only networking behavior that was not related to important career outcomes was that of socializing outside of the workplace. In other words, hanging out with coworkers might build camaraderie

TABLE 8.2. Types of Networking Behaviors

Maintaining Professional Contacts	• Giving out business cards • Sending cards, • using email to communicate
Engaging in Professional Activities	• Attending conferences • Presenting at conferences and local events
Participating in Community Activities	• Attending meetings of civic and social groups • Participating in meetings at a faith community
Increasing Internal Visability	• Accepting new, highly visible work assignments • Going to lunch with your current supervisor
Socializing Outside the Workplace	• Attending social functions within your organization • Playing tennis, golf with your coworkers or clients

(Forret & Dougherty, 2004)

and workplace morale, but doesn't appear to help you advance in your profession. The results of Forret and Dougherty's (2004) research demonstrate a positive relationship between four of the five networking behaviors and the number of promotions. Participants who maintained contacts, engaged in professional activities, participated in community activities, and increased their internal visibility were more likely to be offered promotions.

As you might imagine, promotions are usually accompanied by increases in compensation. Therefore, according to Forret and Dougherty (2004), maintaining external contacts, engaging in professional activities, and increasing internal visibility were positively related to participants' total compensation. Note that the community activities group of networking behaviors is related to promotions, but not salary increases. Likewise, all networking behaviors except community engagement were related to perceived career success. You will learn how to adequately and appropriately document your experiences in both professional and community activities to help you advance in your profession throughout this text.

Interestingly, Forret and Dougherty (2004) found that the effects of some types of interactions differed when they considered gender. For example, increasing internal visibility was only related to the likelihood of promotion for men, but not for women. Similarly, increasing internal visibility was more likely to lead to higher salaries for men, but not for women. Also, for women, the relationship between engaging in professional activities and total compensation was negative; the more women engaged in their profession outside of work, the less they were likely to be paid.

Clearly, there is a relationship between networking behaviors and the opportunities for advancement in the workplace. However, Forret and Dougherty's (2004) results indicate that there is a difference in the utility of networking behaviors for men and women. Gendered strategies for career enhancement are discussed later in this chapter and may provide some insight into these findings.

MODELS OF SOCIAL CAPITAL

Reflect back to the start of this chapter and your invention that will change the world. This time you know who you would contact to have your invention produced, marketed, and financed because you built your network through your internship. However, what type of social capital do you have such that you can call on these contacts to help you out? What will they get in return for helping you out? In other words, how much *social capital do you have?*

FIGURE 8.1. Model of social capital effects on career success

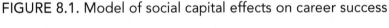

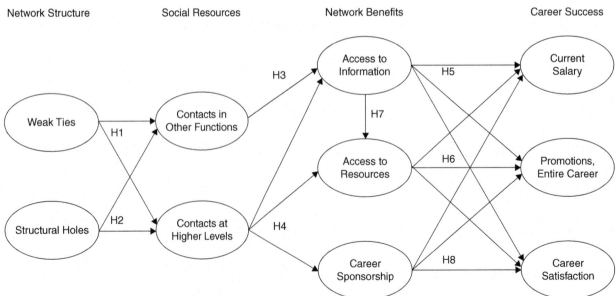

ᵃ Control variables and their paths are not shown for the sake of Clarity. Current salary was a logarithm.

Siebert, Kraimer and Liden (2001) used social capital theory to develop a measurable model of the impact of social networks on organizational (employment) outcomes. Specifically, they investigated network structure, social resources, network benefits, and the relationships between these as they influence organizational outcomes for various groups. Figure 8.1 illustrates the specific elements of their model with both hypothesized relationships and relationships found as a result of their differentiated research.

Clearly social capital is associated with success as it is measured by salary, promotions, and perceived career satisfaction. Though we might have surmised this, Siebert, Kraimer and Liden (2001) demonstrated this using well thought out methodology and research design. Interestingly, their model demonstrates that even weak ties, which we might assume to be related to poor social capital, were positively related to social resources such as number of contacts and contacts at higher levels of their organization. However, these same weak ties were also negatively associated with network benefits such as access to information and career sponsorship. In other words, strong ties are more likely to lead to information and social support for employment and advancement. Conversely, weak ties will help you build social resources, but will not yield career network benefits.

What do Siebert, Kraimer and Liden's (2001) results mean for your networking goals during your internship? During your internship, you should invest in developing weak ties with many others in order to increase your social resources. However, you should be thoughtful and discerning in which of those weak ties you then invest your resources in order to develop stronger ties, likely to be more useful to you in the long run. The Siebert, Kraimer and Liden (2001) model also demonstrates the effects of social capital on organizational outcomes such as promotions, influence and turnover. Specifically, their results indicate support for the role of access to information, resources, and career sponsorship as full mediators of the relations between social capital and career success. Roughly translated, chatting up your coworkers is less effective than investing in relationships that will translate to those coworkers being willing to provide social support in the forms of recommendations about your work ethic, work product, and capabilities. According to their model in Figure 8.1, chatting with key persons at higher levels is instrumental to network benefits and organizational outcomes.

THE VALUE OF WOMEN'S WORK

It is very apparent that Family Science is a female dominated field when we look at the enrollment in our classes. Typically, there are 49 women to each man in the class! Therefore, attention to the gender difference in the process and outcomes of networking behaviors is essential to understanding how to best maximize your opportunities for greater career impact. For example, some of you may have seen videos of a TED talk by Frans de Waal (2011) about what happens when you pay monkeys unequally or a project in Switzerland to honor Equal Pay Day (March 20, 2013). These are comic ways of illustrating the wage differences between men and women and the results of this gap. When we consider that obtaining similar levels of education, similar skill sets, pursuing similar training opportunities, and obtaining mentorship is more beneficial for men than women, it becomes increasingly important to understand ways of circumventing this through networking, a factor within women's control rather than social structure. Pantene's #ShineStrong series highlights the differences between men's and women's approach to their networks, providing a great illustration of how a lack of awareness of women's own social capital can influence other's perceptions of their worth (Bahadur, 2014).

Women have historically been denied access to the 'old boys' network, and therefore they have developed their own. Typically, women's networks tend to be denser, more closed, and more homogenous than those of men. Yet, these dense networks are more likely to be with lower-status individuals and less powerful networks in general (McGuire, 2000; Wang, 2009). In an investigation of the effects of gender and race on social capital, McGuire (2000) found that women and persons of color had lower organizational rank and held positions that were less likely to be in control of key organizational resources.

Despite the fact that their sex or race did not directly affect the status of their network members, female participants and participants of color were less likely than men and Caucasians to have the resources or positions that would put them into contact with high-status employees (McGuire, 2000). Evidence from additional research indicates that there are greater advantages when women develop larger and more diverse social networks. Doing so is more likely to result in greater social capital, higher salaries, more promotions, and greater career satisfaction (Seibert, Kaimer, & Liden, 2001) as discussed in the previous section.

Unfortunately, several challenges impede women's attempts to build strong, effective networks. First, women have been shown to have less access to informal networks than their male counterparts (Forret & Dougherty, 2004). Women's lack of access to informal networks results in greater difficulty breaking into more powerful male-dominated networks. Another hypothesized reason for the challenges facing women in their attempts to build professional networks is the fact that they have less time outside of work due to more family responsibilities (Linehan & Scullion, 2008). Also, female mentors are either in short supply in some environments or due to their additional responsibilities outside of work, have less time available to mentor women who would like to advance in their field. In addition, high-ranking men are more likely to become mentors for other men due to their comfort in developing professional and personal relationships with other men (Ehrich, 1994). Though we often think of the Second Shift work as having been solved in the past 20 years, the research on women's networks in the past decade demonstrate that this issue has not been resolved.

In a series of studies examining networking behaviors, researchers found that gender, socioeconomic background, extraversion, self-esteem and attitudes about workplace politics were related to networking behaviors (Forret & Dougherty, 2001; 2004). Despite the popular misconception that women are more social, these results indicated that men spent more time socializing than the women in the study. However, when men and *single* women were compared, there were no differences in the amount of socializing between these two groups. These results indicate that gender plays less of a role in socializing as a networking behavior than does relationship status (Forret & Dougherty, 2001).

Forret and Dougherty's (2004) results, discussed in detail in an earlier section, clearly indicate that networking behaviors are more directly related to success, as measured by number of promotions and total compensation, for men than they are for women. These results might be explained through further analysis of the types of committees, task forces, and assignments given to women. It may also be related to the fact that women are less likely to ask for a pay increase (Wellington & Catalyst, 2001) and have lesser access to influential persons within their networks (Dreher & Cox, 2000). Given the results of the body of literature examining the moderating effect of gender on networking behaviors, students in Family Science would benefit greatly from attending to the upcoming section on *how* to network and map their social capital. By doing so, you will greatly increase your career opportunities after graduation as well as increase the likelihood of advancing in your organization once you are employed.

How to Network

In Forbes magazine's list of 6 things you MUST do to get your first job after college, networking and internship are referenced in every item.

1. Create a LinkedIn profile.
2. Establish a presence on WordPress or through your own blog.
3. Get an internship as early as possible.
4. Get creative about finding a mentor.
5. Use your school's career services office.
6. Join a professional development or industry specific group.

(Adapted from Adams, S. (November 12, 2012). 6 things you must do to get your first job after college, Retrieved from http://www.forbes.com/sites/susanadams/2012/11/12/6-things-you-must-do-to-get-your-first-job-after-college/)

How to Network on Your Internship

Networking as an Intern

This list of pointers/guidelines specifically for interns about how to network has been assembled from successful professionals and career experts.

1. Remember names and faces. This cultivates the impression that you are detail-oriented, conscientious, and motivated.
2. Be sincere. Don't misrepresent what you do and don't know—you are an intern and are expected to be learning during your internship.
3. Find some face time. You are more likely to get a good project or a job offer if someone knows your face versus your profile.
4. Join the Big Kid activities. Spend time with those in charge, not just other interns.
5. Show up alone. By attending work events by yourself, you will be forced to mingle with your professional contacts rather than rely on your friends/date.
6. Skip the email. Keep in touch with coworkers and supervisors via email related to tasks you are given to complete. However, a quick hello or short chat will provide you more face time (see #3) so they get to know you outside of those tasks.
7. Save the tough ones for the last. Being an intern can be intimidating; some coworkers or supervisors can be intimidating too. Reach out to the easiest ones first to gain confidence.
8. Evaluate them. Pay attention to whether or not the organization is a good fit for you and your professional goals to help you streamline your ideas about potential employers after graduation.

(Adapted from: Dizik, A. (June 18, 2007). Networking for Interns. Bloomberg BusinessWeek. Retrieved from

http://www.businessweek.com/stories/2007-06-18/networking-for-internsbusinessweek-business-news-stock-market-and-financial-advice)

As an intern, you might be more concerned with learning *how* to do your tasks for your internship rather than how to make the most of your internship as a networking opportunity. Luckily, this chapter provides you with an overview of how to network as an intern as well as a method for deciding upon your networking goals before you actually start your internship experience. If you are reading this text, you've already taken significant steps in building your professional network—thinking about professionalism and deciding to do an internship!

The following section lists several items to be aware of in terms of building your connections to key others during your internship experience. While it may be more comfortable to go with the familiar—an internship in your hometown or one with an agency where you have volunteered for the past 3 years— we strongly encourage you to extend your goals beyond your comfort zone. An internship is a relatively short time commitment and will give you the opportunity to explore your opportunities with very little risk! If you do decide to go with the familiar, make sure that you really take advantage of the opportunity to engage with high-status professionals and key others that will help you build your network through your internship. This is especially true if you intend to live in that community when you graduate.

You can increase your connections with your formal networks through joining your professional organization or student association early in your academic career. Most majors have student associations within the department to help students with similar professional interests build their connections, to each other and to their professional community. The National Council on Family Relations (NCFR) is home to many Family Science-related professionals, both academic and practicing, and as we have mentioned, undergraduate students are eligible for a student membership. This organization is a great example of how to begin to make connections in the professional world before graduation. Additionally, you may want to take on leadership roles within your student organization (Felson, 2001) or volunteer with a local, regional, or national professional organization in order to gain exposure to professionals in your field. NCFR has added incentives for undergraduates such as the NCFR Honors Recognition program in which you can be formally acknowledged for your academic excellence and leadership through a stole at graduation, recognition throughout the membership in the NCFR Report, and recognition at the annual NCFR conference. This is an excellent return on investment and will significantly increase your visibility in terms of job searching with other professionals in Family Science.

As an intern, you are encouraged to cast your net widely. As research reviewed in this chapter found, many weak ties can be related to greater visibility and greater employment options later. For example, most students come to Family Science fields by accident or later in their academic careers because they didn't know this discipline existed in the shadow of the social science juggernauts of psychology and sociology. You didn't know what a great fit Family Science would be until you found it; the same is likely true for an internship site and a potential employer, so look far and wide!

Follow up with people you meet through your current network. You can do this by making inexpensive business cards with your name, contact information, your **professional** email address, and the URL to your personal webpage (Felson, 2001). By doing so, you increase others' perceptions of your professionalism and you have a card to hand out when professionals hand you theirs.

Multiple Internships = Exponential advantages!

Many programs and disciplines do not give or require course credit for internships, yet students are expected to take the initiative to seek out internships on their own to help them to be more competitive for jobs (business, finance, marketing, public relations, etc). If you are fortunate enough to have your degree-related work experience count toward your education, consider it doubly beneficial. But your degree-related work experience is valuable even if it doesn't contribute toward your graduation credits. In fact, you should still take the opportunity to intern, build your network and build your work experience in a career-related field because employers are rarely interested in what courses you took, but rather what skills and experiences you have had. Consider multiple internships across multiple sites, some paid, some for credit and some as a volunteer internships in order to build your network, try out different work environments, contribute to your field and your community, or just to gain the experience! Make sure you balance your GPA and your applied experiences though; don't pursue internships at the expense of doing well in your courses.

ONLINE NETWORKING

This text has successfully made the case that your digital identity is an essential component of your professional development in the chapter on digital identity. Clearly, building your connections in your professional life through virtual means has definite advantages. Networking online allows you to increase your audience and adds flexibility to where and when you can network (McCarty, 2006). Long gone are the days when you had to wait for the next conference or meeting in order to be able to connect with colleagues, collaborators, or supervisors.

Networking through virtual means supplements the face-time you have with important contacts. Notice we said *supplements* face-time. As an intern and a new professional, you need to put in adequate face-time to build enough of a connection to then have an online, networked relationship. Experts advise employees to use the same logic and consideration online that you would in an in-person meeting (Feldstein, 2012). This means that you should get to know individuals and establish some common ground through your in-person interactions before trying to connect with them online.

LinkedIn is a popular professional networking site that can be used to help you build your formal, career, and task networks. This site allows you to link to people you know and would like to continue relationships with and provides an excellent way to keep your personal digital identity separate from your professional digital identity. As an intern, you can use LinkedIn to introduce yourself to others through a mutual connection. This is a good way to build the density of your network and connect with higher-status individuals through your current network.

LinkedIn has demonstrated its value as a networking resource to students. When students are assigned networking as a part of their semester grade, results indicate that students found it to be both useful and beneficial (Peterson & Dover, 2014). Specifically, students were required to create LinkedIn accounts and complete various other requirements throughout the semester. For example, students were required to complete an all-star level of their profile to include photo, work history, skills, and so forth; build a minimum of 20 new connections, half of which were to be professional connections; join at least five groups; post a question/comment in these groups at least five times; and write one letter of recommendation for a connection and receive one letter of recommendation written by a second connection (Peterson & Dover, 2014).

The results indicated that students engaged in their LinkedIn connections beyond what was required. Additionally, students reported job opportunities that became available to them through their participation on LinkedIn (Peterson & Dover, 2014). Their participation in LinkedIn over the course of the semester helped them become more confident in networking online and become aware of the utility of the site, and helped them learn how to use these tools to develop their digital identity.

Other experts offer advice on how to maximize your online networking efforts. For example, "It's not a numbers race. You want to build quality, ongoing relationships" (Feldstein, 2012, p. 73). One way to ensure that you are building quality relationships is to recommend and endorse only those people with whom you have actually worked. Recommendations and endorsements via LinkedIn act as a vetting system and if you are vouching for someone and they aren't competent, then it is your reputation at stake. Also, customize your invitations to be connected with a short, personal note, preferably one in which you reference a mutual connection or interest.

Similarly, only ask for recommendations and endorsements from those with whom you have a working relationship. By asking for a recommendation from someone who has not worked with you or doesn't really know the quality of your work, you are putting the reference on the spot. Making a potential resource uncomfortable is a good way to alienate that person for future interactions. It is important that you cultivate positive interactions with your professional network.

While using sites such as LinkedIn will help you maintain your external contacts, it is important to remember that as an intern or a new professional, you still have to prove yourself to others in order for them to assist you in meeting your professional goals. The information in this chapter can be condensed down to its take-home points: use specific networking behaviors to develop many weak ties during your internship, both in person and online; decide which of these relationships you should invest in to reap the greatest impact on your career and employment options; and create networking goals for your internship using the guidelines provided in Chapter 8 on using social media appropriately.

MAPPING YOUR SOCIAL CAPITAL

Go back to the Chapter 1 Life Map Activity where you identified your personal, professional, and civic identities. Using the Life Map you created:	
1. Fill in your additional network connections with specific names of individuals who fall within:	- personal networks - professional networks - civic networks Draw connections between others that know each other as well, to determine the density of your network
2. color code your networks according to the types discussed in this chapter:	- formal - informal - community-based - task - career - social support
3. After filling out the diagram, notice the following:	a) How many and how strong are the connections? b) Which of your types of networks contain the strongest ties? The most ties? c) What is the status of the individuals who comprise your professional network? d) Are there gaps in your work-related networks? e) What is the density of your work-related networks? In other words, how many connection crossovers are there?

What steps can you take to fill in the career-related gaps in your network?
Create at least five goals to accomplish these during your internship.

1.

2.

3.

4.

5.

Assess your social resources and network to help you rate the level of social capital in your network.	
For those you identified as part of your professional network, rate the status of the connections on your Life Map.	• Put a 0 next to the ones that are peer relationships in which you are at an approximately equal status. Put a +1 next to those that would be your supervisors and a +2 for your supervisors' supervisors (even if you are only connected through your immediate supervisor). Put a −1 for those that you supervise or who report to you.

Review your network looking for connections to foster and develop. List at least 3 areas/ relationships where you should add connections and list at least two strategies for developing these connections during your internship for each area/relationship.

Area/Relationship to add connections	Strategies for accomplishing the connection
1.	a. b.
2.	a. b.
3.	a. b.

Successful Self Promotion Strategies	
1. Elevator Speech	Edit your elevator speech frequently to highlight what is new and exciting with your work. This could include new opportunities, and programs or projects you are involved in through your internship site.

Write a draft of your elevator speech using the space provided. In 2–3 sentences summarize your experiences, skills, and how these relate to your career goals.

2. Build your professional network	As an intern, pay attention to the individuals you meet through your internship and make it a point to meet others who interact with your internship site. Take the initiative to let these individuals know what you learned from meeting them.

Write five different informal ways you can network during your internship (e.g. write a brief thank you email for suggesting an important resource).

a.

b.

c.

d.

e.

3. Join your professional organization	If you haven't already, make sure you join your professional organization and/or student associations linked to your field. These give you a great opportunity to be invited to listen to guest speakers to give you more chances to network.

List at least two professional organizations and two student associations or clubs that are relevant to your career choices.

Professional Organizations:

a.

b.

Student organizations/Clubs

a.

b.

4. Take the Arm & Hammer approach	Originally used for baking, it is now used for cleaning, deodorizing, and even whitening teeth! Use your creativity and innovation to find additional ways to use existing products, programs, and projects!

Use this space to explain at least one creative, innovative way you have contributed to a workplace, a project, or group.

5. Volunteer	Maximize your skills and strengths to volunteer your time in a highly visible way. Use your volunteerism as a way to network with key decision makers during your internship or in your community. Use these interactions as opportunities to advance professionally, not just to socialize.

Describe at least three ways your volunteer experiences translate to your professional skills or qualities you can bring to an internship site.

a.

b.

c.

6. Be a mentor	Share your knowledge and expertise with others. As an intern, this could be giving back to your department or program by being a panelist for future interns to learn about your experience. This is also a great way to cultivate relationships with your peers who will likely be in other organizations and a great way to build your network!

List at least three organizations or group *outside of the university/college* where you can contribute by being a mentor.

a.

b.

c.

(From Shakur, L. (2003). Don't keep yourself a secret. *OfficePro*, 63(3), 6–8.

REFERENCES

Abel, J., Dietz, R., & Su, Y. (2014). Are Recent College Graduates Finding Jobs. Current issues in Economics and Finance, 20 (1), 1–8.

Adams, S. (November 12, 2012). 6 Things You Must Do To Get Your First Job After College. Retrieved from http://www.forbes.com/sites/susanadams/2012/11/12/6-things-you-must-do-to-get-your-first-job-after-college/

Adecco Staffing. (May 9, 2013). Hiring Managers Believe New College Grads Are Unprepared For The Workplace. Retrieved from http://www.adeccousa.com/articles/Hiring-Managers-Believe-New-College-Grads-are-Unprepared-for-the-Workforce.html?id=215&url=/pressroom/pressreleases/pages/forms/allitems.aspx&templateurl=/AboutUs/pressroom/Pages/Press-release.aspx

Bahadur, N. (June 18, 2014). Pantene 'Not Sorry' video tells women to stop apologizing so much. Retrieved from http://www.huffingtonpost.com/2014/06/18/pantene-not-sorry-shine-strong_n_5507461.html

Bradford, S. (2005). Experts Offer Their Tips for fruitful networking. Wall street Journal, Executive Career Site. Retrieved from www.careerjournaleurope.com/jobhunting/networking/20050215-bradford.html

de Waal, F. (2011). Moral behavior in animals. Presented at TEDx Peachtree. Retrieved from http://www.ted.com/talks/frans_de_waal_do_animals_have_morals

Dizik, A. (June 18, 2007). Networking for Interns. *Bloomberg BusinessWeek*. Retrieved from http://www.businessweek.com/stories/2007-06-18/networking-for-internsbusinessweek-business-news-stock-market-and-financial-advice

Dreher, G. & Cox, T. (2000). Labor Market Mobility And Cash Compensation: The Moderating Effects Of Race And Gender. *Academy of Management Journal, 43*, 890–900.

Ehrich, L.C. (1994). Mentoring and networking for women educators. *Women in Management Review, 9(3)*, 4–10.

Equal Pay Day (March 20, 2013). Retrieved from (https://www.youtube.com/watch?v=ZcAOwYmpZW4)

Feldstein, M. (2012). Are You Building Strong Career Relationships. *T+D, 66(12)*, 72–73.

Felson, L. (2001). Undergrad marketers must get jump on networking skills. *Marketing News, 35(8)*, 14–15.

Forret, M.L. & Dougherty, T.W. (2001). Correlates of networking behavior for managerial and professional employees. *Group and Organization Management, 26*, 283–311.

Forret, M.L. & Dougherty, T.W. (2004). Neworking behaviors and career outcomes: Differences for men and women. *Journal of Organizational Behavior, 25(3)*, 419–437

Garavan, T., Hogan, C. & Cahir-O'Donnell, A. (2003). *Making Training and Development work: A best practice guide*. Dublin; Oak Tree Press.

Ibarra, H. (1995). Race opportunity, and diversity of social circles in managerial networks. *Academy of Management Journal, 38*, 673–703.

Linehan, M. & Scullion, H. (2008). The development of female globa l managers: The role of mentoring and networking. *Journal of Business Ethics, 83*, 29–40.

McCarty, M. (2006). Who needs to network? *OfficePro, 66(6)*, 24–26.

McGuire, G. (2000). Gender, Race, Ethnicity, And Networks: The Factors Affecting The Status Of Employees' Networks Members. *Work and Occupations, 27, 4*, 501–524.

Peterson, R. & Dover, H. (2014). Building student networks with LinkedIn: the potential for connections, internships, and jobs. *Marketing Education Review, 24, 1*, 15–20.

Seibert, S.E., Kraimer, M.L. & Liden, R.C. (2001). A Social Capital Theory of Career Success. *Academy of Management Journal, 44*, 219–237.

Shakur, L. (2003). Don't keep yourself a secret. *OfficePro, 63(3)*, 6–8.

Wang, J. (2009). Networking in the workplace: Implications for women's career development. *New Directions for Adult and Continuing Education, 122*, 33–42.

Wellington, S. & Catalyst. (2001). *Be your own mentor*. New York: Random House.

9

What does Community Mean to You?

OBJECTIVES

By the end of this chapter you should be able to:

➤ Define community
➤ Identify communities
➤ Understand how to build community
➤ Understand how to engage with communities
➤ Understand how to develop a civic identity

In the first chapter, you read about civic, or community identity, remember? Reach into your bag or folder and resurrect the Life Map activity (Hall, 2010) that you completed. What communities did you identify as being a member of? Why? And why are they important to you? You probably identified communities that are represented by people, places or something else entirely. Most likely, you identified communities in which you have both active and passive roles. As an active participant, you engage with people and/or places to take a stand or make a difference. For example, you may be the President, Vice President, Secretary, or Treasurer of a leadership group or organization. On the other hand, you may just attend meetings when your schedule permits.

THINK ABOUT IT.

What physical locations and people are represented in your Life Map? Use the table below to list the locations and people, and whether or not they evoke positive or negative associations.

Positive Associations	Negative Associations

Review the list and think about whether any of these locations are suitable for professional experiences, like internships. Is there something more you can gain from seeking an internship in a place that stirs negativity? You may determine that challenging yourself allows for significant growth; do not dismiss it. Similarly, are there people you identified who you could utilize to grow professionally? They represent many networks that you can access to make connections, as you learned in Chapter 8.

Technically, you may still consider yourself a part of the group, but you have a passive role in it. To get the most out of your internship, you should understand the internship community and seek to be an active member of it. But how do you do that? In many cases, the physical location may be limited by the location of your university. If you have the opportunity to go beyond that, will you seek opportunities closer to home, or spread your wings and explore another area entirely? Wherever you decide to go, this chapter will help you understand why you need to understand where you are going, and who you will interact with when you get there.

How to Build Community

Before you can build community, you have to define it. Take a moment and jot down your answers the questions:

1. What is community?
2. What does it mean to you?

According to some, a community is a place where individuals look out for themselves and others (Anderson & Milligan, 2006). As an intern and emerging professional, this means that you need to be aware of your goals and place within your internship, and any other relevant community that you interact with during your experience. Another way of thinking about community could involve culture. Culture can be defined as "attitudes, behaviors, and symbols shared by a large group of people and usually communicated from one generation to the next" (Shiraev & Levy, 2010, p. 23). You learn these things within a community, which can take the form of a country, state, or region, a neighborhood or local community, an institution that house people (school, classroom, and workplace), a racial, ethnic, or religious group, or any set of like-minded people with whom one identifies. With that very encompassing definition, community is essentially *anything you define* as being important to your socialization, or how you learn about the world.

So, now that you have a definition of community, how do you go about building it? As a relative newcomer to the internship community, you must learn how to look out for yourself and for others. To do this, you need to pay attention to the way the community works, and who works within it. If you did a scholarly search on community building, you would locate articles on community capacity and social capital, two terms that will help you understand how to build and engage in community.

The concepts of social capital and community capacity are important to your experience because social capital is about the process of an organization or agency working with individuals towards a shared common goal, while community capacity is built because of that process (Anderson & Milligan, 2006). "According to the most widely accepted definitions, social capital captures qualities inherent in social relationships—such as trust, shared norms and values—that arise in social groups and promote social organization, cooperation, and collective action for the common good" (Anderson & Milligan, 2006, p. 22). This is not entirely different from the definition of culture, but the emphasis is placed on shared trust and values with community capacity, characteristics that are personal in nature and rely on cooperation of individuals as they interact with each other within the community. This is what we commonly refer to as a sense of community; a place or a group of people that makes you feel comforted, heard, and not alone (Anderson & Milligan, 2006). The community, then, can be viewed as a system, just like a family, with interconnected and reciprocal parts that are in a constant state of change (Anderson & Sabatelli, 2006). As an intern, you become a part of this system and you have an opportunity to learn from others, hopefully building up your strengths through mutually beneficial relationships. You provide a fresh perspective and display a willingness to learn, while individuals in the internship placement commit to providing an educational experience that enables you to learn valuable, translatable professional skills.

But how do you know that the internship you find will provide an opportunity for you to learn about community and gain new skills? You must use the research you began in Chapter 3 to make a fully informed decision. Due to the plugged-in nature of the world, agencies and organizations have not only been able to utilize their local community more efficiently, but also expand their reach into other place based, or interest-based communities to gain a foothold and create more opportunities for positive change. As an intern, it is important that you understand the role that technology and the internet can play in your experience, as well as the potential for skill growth.

In your research to learn more about an agency or organization for an internship, you should have searched their website. To find the placement, you might have utilized the United Way in your community, or looked through Volunteer.org or Idealist.org. All of these websites allow agencies to build new communities of supporters, which was much harder to do in past decades. Now, you can not only find the information you are seeking through these sites, but more importantly, you can also find out how to help become a part of their mission and engage new community members (Boeder, 2002).

As you explore your options, it is important to understand the power that you have over your experience. Another important aspect of building community is what is called 'Psychological Sense of Community', which means that you feel you belong, have influence, can be influenced, can learn, and that you can become invested in not only your experience, but also invested in the internship placement (Anderson & Milligan, 2006). Thus, finding the right fit for your personal and professional needs relies heavily on you.

You have the power to arm yourself with the knowledge you need and make the decision that allows you to grow in the manner you seek. At the end of the day, you make the experience what it is. You have already thought about who you are, so how do you learn more about the community a potential placement is located in? Completing a demographic profile of a place-based community can allow you to identify sources of strength and weaknesses, and also those of interest to you. After completing the *Demographic Profile* in the *Applying Your Knowledge* section of this chapter, perhaps you determine that a majority of the population is above the age of 50, but a majority of the services offered are for children under the age of 10. What could you do about this in your internship? You can explore the agencies that do serve the aging population and work to help them build their own community capacity to expand their outreach capabilities.

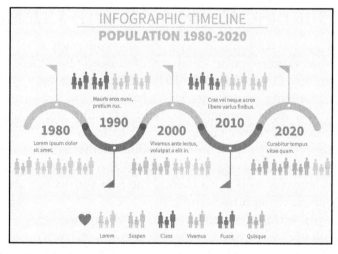

© 2015 by microvector. Used under license of Shutterstock, Inc.

Building Community with Colleagues

To build community with colleagues, here are a few reminders.

- Understand the type of communication that occurs in your internship site. Is it top-down or is everyone involved?
- Do the research. Be a "Go To" intern.
- Ask questions.
- Be the first to share a mistake—it is okay!
- Give input. Remember, you're not "just an intern."

© 2015 by Goodluz. Used under license of Shutterstock, Inc.

If you communicate professionally and follow the recommendations in Chapter 5, you have taken the first steps to building community with those you will work with during your internship. The next step is gaining knowledge of who your colleagues are in your internship. How long have they been there? What is their educational background? What do they expect you to do? And most importantly, what working style will they employ with you?

Most supervisors will fall under one of the three types of supervisory roles: nondirective, collaborative and directive (Slick, 2000).

- Nondirective: Uses active listening and asks many questions to allow an intern to solve problems on their own, assuming that the intern has the knowledge to do so.
- Collaborative: Uses active listening skills and asks many questions, but solves problems with the intern to determine the right course of action, assuming that the intern does not yet have the knowledge to do so.
- Directive: Uses direction to solve problems, and does not ask questions of the intern.

Although many supervisors may have a general supervisory style, there is fluidity. Think about a supervisor in a shelter for victims of domestic violence. They may be very collaborative on a *normal* day, but when a client walks in experiencing an immediate crisis, their style may shift to a directive approach because it fits the situation (Slick, 2000). To learn more about a potential supervisor, ask them the questions above, and make a list of additional questions that you have.

Make a list of questions you have for supervisors. Use the answers to help you determine whether or not you feel a sense of community, or feel as if you could work well with them during your internship.

BUILDING COMMUNITY WITH CLIENTS

To build community with clients, you must first know who they are as people. Reflect on the observations you made about the image of a female and a child in Chapter 1, as well as the results of your Project Implicit (2011) test. Any chance of building community with clients will be lost if you make assumptions about who they are, instead of simply taking the time to learn more about them. Apart from knowing clients, your approach in working with them also matters. When you work with clients, the role you have defines the approach you take.

It is important to be aware of the diversity of roles because just like supervisory roles, each one has its place. Additionally, the role that you take on reflects your assumptions, biases and goals. In Family Life Education, the following types of roles exist (Duncan & Goddard, 2011).

- Expert: Clients are uninformed and therefore, there to receive knowledge.
- Facilitator: Clients are informed, but are there to have someone help them utilize their potential.
- Critical Inquirer: Clients have a responsibility to contribute to society, so they are there to have someone ask them questions about how they can help.
- Collaborator: Clients have lived experiences and the collaborator has educational background and experience. They work together to problem solve.

- Interventionist: Clients need assistance and are there to have someone provide a plan of action that will be evaluated and help clients change attitudes or behaviors.
- Eclectic: This approach can be a combination of any of the roles, depending on the goodness of fit for the situation.

Regardless of the role, it is important to know that the most effective way of building community with clients and engaging them in their own futures, is to empower them. Instead of providing, or pushing, answers or decisions, enable them to recognize their own (Anderson & Milligan, 2006). You can be invested in their decision making process without solving their problems for them. Remember, you will be gone one day, and you want to be confident that they can thrive without assistance.

One way to do this is to ensure that their needs are met. As a student in a Human Services department, you have surely learned about Maslow's Hierarchy of Needs. You may be thinking: what does that have to do with building community with clients? Well, think about it for a moment. Maslow (1968) proposed that in order for individuals to reach self-actualization, the final stage of human development,

HIERARCHY OF NEEDS
by Abraham Maslow

they must first have their physiological, safety, social and esteem needs met. When working with clients, the first thing to understand is why they are there and what their goals are in using the services. For example, how is a client working to regain custody of a child different from or similar to a client working to obtain his or her GED?

According to Maslow, a client who is willing to move forward in his or her development feels safe, while a client who is unwilling or disengaged in the process does not have their needs met. So what can you do to work with that client? Well, you need to know your boundaries and work within the rules, regulations and abilities of the agency or organization to provide necessary resources. With all of the information that you have learned about yourself and others, what theories can you apply to provide context and understanding for your community?

Community building will not solve all of the problems that may occur, or challenges that arise, but it will provide a space in which people feel comfortable sharing their triumphs and struggles. These people not only include colleagues and clients, but also you. A sense of community will be the idea, or feeling, that enables people to utilize an agency or organization because they know they have tools to succeed (Anderson & Milligan, 2006). You will encounter diverse situations, and you may need to employ other theories that you have learned to understand the situation. What other theories/theorists can you read and study about to better understand yourself, the community, and the experience you are interested in learning more about?

During your internship, you will learn to utilize skills that represent your strengths, and you will also have the opportunity to develop your weaknesses into strengths as you learn about communication, leadership, and organizational skills, just to name a few. In Chapter 4, communication is addressed, but it is important to remember that you must set that stage for learning as much as you can in your internship. One way you can do this is through leadership. Surely you have heard that leadership is important, but why? In college, you have undoubtedly been told to get involved in student organizations, on or off campus to build your leadership skills. But what is leadership? Before we discuss it further, take a moment to reflect on what leadership means to you.

What is leadership?
What are some barriers to leadership?
How are you a leader?
Why are you a leader?

© 2015 by Rawpixel. Used under license of Shutterstock, Inc.

In most literature, leadership is defined by either an industrialist or a post-industrialist paradigm (Shertzer & Schuh, 2004). The primary distinction is that an industrialist definition is about an individual being a leader for others, whereas the post-industrialist definition is about individuals working together for change. As we discussed above, a post-industrialist perspective of leadership fits into our discussion of building community. As a new intern, you will have many opportunities to develop leadership skills in yourself and in others. According to a study of college students in leadership positions, as well as those disengaged in the campus community, by Shertzer and Schuh (2004), students reported four primary types of leadership: individual possession, positional, specific qualities and skills, and internal motivations.

- Individual possession: A single person is most likely a natural leader, but in some cases may be able to develop the necessary skills to be a special person capable of leadership.
- Positional: A specific position is necessary to lead others, e.g. President, Vice President, etc.
- Specific skills and qualities: Students who are leaders note that extroverts who are able to persuade and motivate others to do things make for better leaders. Those disengaged believed that introverts can work well behind the scenes.
- Internal motivations: People are in leadership positions to work with others, personal development and passion for the organization.

As you can see, taken together, these characteristics of leadership allow individuals to gain personal and professional skills while working with others for the good of an organization or agency, but in very different ways. Students in the study also noted the importance of support from others and having experience in leadership to be a truly effective leader (Shertzer & Schuh, 2004). Review your thoughts on leadership; did you list qualities that the students mentioned? What barriers did you include?

Often, transitioning into an internship position and finding your place within an organization can be difficult, making the prospect of leadership even scarier than it was before! As you develop relationships in a new environment and gain professional experiences, you will gain confidence, one of the main factors in being a successful leader (Shertzer & Schuh, 2004).

In Chapter 1, you listed your strengths and weaknesses. Use the space below to record the specific qualities you have related to leadership.

Strengths	Weaknesses

Based on the list above, think about how you are qualified to be a leader.

How can you develop your weaknesses into strengths that enable you to be a leader? Another way to think about this is by assessing what characteristics represent opportunities and threats to your success?

Opportunities	Threats

How can you be a resource for others to be a leader, e.g. clients in your internship?

How to Engage in Community

The first step in engaging with a community is to understand it. You have to unpack your assumptions and biases and actually learn about where you are going. Review the image from Chapter 1 and your initial feelings. How would you feel if you were that person being judged by your environment? Would you be willing to engage with the person passing the judgment? Would you be willing to learn about ways you could improve your environment? Probably not. As you read through the rest of this chapter, remember

to keep your strengths-based perspective at the forefront, and think about how much more enjoyable and eventful life can be when you accomplish things with others—that is, with a community.

To make the most of your internship, or any future professional experience, you must be willing to think about your assumptions and check them at the door. Get to know an organization and the people within it before rushing to a judgment. You will never learn if you do not do so, and you will certainly be miserable. Instead, do the research and ask questions, and take advantage of the opportunity that you have through your program to make explicit connections between what you have learned in school, and what is happening in the *real world*. Creating connections between what is happening beyond the university walls and the community will help you gain a greater understanding of the impact that you can have on the world. It also allows you to form relationships within the community, an important aspect of the work in human services (Malone & Tranter, 2003), as well as a way in which to develop leadership opportunities.

One of the most important lessons to learn is that community engagement means taking a "do with" approach instead of a "do-to" or a "do-for" one (Okubo & Weidman, 2000). To engage the community, you must be willing to listen. As an intern, this means that you must listen to yourself, colleagues and clients. In Chapter 1, you learned about cultural competencies during your internship—the idea that you are constantly aware of yourself and those around you. In Chapter 4, you worked on defining your personal learning objectives and developing goals. As you actually work towards your goals, you must keep others in mind. Although the goal is for you to have a positive learning experience during your internship, you are working in the field with others who will remain there long after you leave. You must make sure that you take a "do-with" approach to ensure that you are not leaving behind something that will not exist or thrive without you because no one really wanted it in the first place.

Review your Demographic Profile activity and reflect on the ways you recorded you could help in the community. Keep that in your mind, and we will come back to it in a moment after reviewing the National Council on Family Relations (2011) Content Areas for Family Life Educators. The content areas represent the breadth and depth of knowledge that you receive as a student in a human services oriented department and can assist you in determining what interests you may want to pursue in an internship—those areas that can help you build and engage in community.

1. Families and Individuals in Societal Contexts: An understanding of families and their relationships to other institutions, such as the educational, governmental, religious, and occupational institutions in society.
2. Internal Dynamics of Families: An understanding of family strengths and weaknesses and how family members relate to each other.
3. Human Growth and Development Across the Lifespan: An understanding of the developmental changes of individuals in families throughout the lifespan. Based on knowledge of physical, emotional, cognitive, social, moral, and personality aspects.

4. Human Sexuality: An understanding of the physiological, psychological, & social aspects of sexual development throughout the lifespan, so as to achieve healthy sexual adjustment.
5. Interpersonal Relationships: An understanding of the development and maintenance of interpersonal relationships.
6. Family Resource Management: An understanding of the decisions individuals and families make about developing and allocating resources including time, money, material assets, energy, friends, neighbors, and space, to meet their goals.
7. Parent Education and Guidance: An understanding of how parents teach, guide and influence children and adolescents as well as the changing nature, dynamics and needs of the parent/child relationship across the lifespan.
8. Family Law and Public Policy: An understanding of the legal issues, policies, and law influencing the well-being of families.
9. Professional Ethics and Practice: An understanding of the character and quality of human social conduct, and the ability to critically examine ethical questions and issues as they relate to professional practice.
10. Family Life Education Methodology: An understanding of the general philosophy and broad principles of family life education in conjunction with the ability to plan, implement, and evaluate such educational programs.

National Council on Family Relations. www.ncfr.org. 888-781-9331. Reprinted with permission.

Now that you have reviewed the content areas, record those that you find the most interesting and could see yourself learning more about in a field-based internship. Before you begin your internship, what can you do to learn more about the content areas now? You can start by searching at least one of the following websites: United Way, Volunteer.org, or Idealist.org. Use a search term related to the NCFR content areas that you selected as an area of interest. What results do you get?

Now, let's go back to your Demographic Profile. What did you identify as an issue, or a solution? Although we have discussed how to build and engage community, you must do your research because you have to acknowledge the work that is already happening within the community. You are probably not the first one to identify an issue or a solution, so who else is already working on it? You must be willing to identify all stakeholders, get buy-in, engage all stakeholders, and be flexible. It is also important to truly identify all stakeholders—not only those that can help, but also those that can hinder. Identify at least one trend from your *Demographic Profile*, and think about how the organizations in the community can be involved in this issue. Be informed so that you can become a more engaged member of the community (Okubo & Weidman, 2000).

HOW TO DEVELOP A CIVIC IDENTITY

Now that you understand more about building and engaging in community, how do you use that information to develop a civic identity, and what does that mean? To help you become a steward of your community, you first need a sense of place there and an opportunity to learn about what working in the community means to/for you. An internship is "holistic, integrated, and meaningful, thereby facilitating the development... [your] knowledge, skills, and dispositions towards the local culture," or community (Embersole & Worster, 2007, p. 2). You will learn contextual information about the environment or

PEOPLE

circumstance, e.g. SES, neighborhood safety, family structure in your internship. In the previous sections of this chapter, you have explored some of this information as you thought about your place within the community, whether it be directly at your internship, or with those people your internship provides services to in their community. We hope that you use your skill set and/or goals to redefine the measure of success beyond grades and towards social justice. Throughout your internship, you will become invested in that community and gain cultural competency, which will enable you to continuously think critically and reflexively on your personal identities, and the identity of the community where you are learning and experiencing the world. In diverse forms, you will become a social steward who is civically engaged in the community. You may even hope to remain there to continue the work you have started, or you may hope to return one day. After your experience, you should be even more aware of all that your community has to offer, something you may not have been as aware of before the internship began.

By building and engaging in community, you are being civically responsible, which "entails participation in activities that seek to enhance the quality of the overall society and its diverse constituents, not simply one's own life or the lives of one's immediate circle" (Singer, King, Green, & Barr, 2002, p. 536). Undoubtedly, the work of building and engaging in community is not without challenges. As you struggle and experience triumphs, you will be more likely to become invested in the process and the people, developing a civic identity.

Throughout our years of working with students in internships, we have observed this development process. In the beginning, the students are excited about learning. Then, they encounter a situation that challenges their notion of success, and of their role within it. They doubt themselves and wonder how they can ever pursue a career in the field. Fortunately, they are surrounded by seasoned community members who reiterate that success is in the eye of the beholder. Success is what you make of it. Focusing on the outcome can be daunting, but focusing on the process of growth can be inspiring. We share this anecdote to emphasize the notion that you are in control of your experience. The level of your investment is up to you, but the more you invest, the more will you gain.

When you leave your internship, what impression do you want to leave behind?

In a study of young adults, researchers found that many had generative thoughts (McAdams, de St. Aubin, & Logan, 1993). You may recognize this concept from your studies of Erikson—the idea that older adults seek to leave a legacy to future generations. Interestingly, although the young adults felt generative, they were not as likely to take action on making their thoughts a reality, unlike their older peers in middle adulthood (McAdams, de St. Aubin, & Logan, 1993). To understand why, researchers compared the experiences of college seniors participating in service learning versus experiences in banks or magazines. The researchers found that students engaged in service learning in community-based organizations/agencies did take generative actions. They were more likely than their peers in non-human services placements to connect their personal growth to their placements and their community (Singer, King, Green, & Barr, 2002). These findings demonstrate that it is possible that your experiences in an internship will lead you to have similar feelings. Not only will you ask what kind of impression you want to leave, but you will ask how—and you will make it happen.

Through your efforts of building and engaging community, you will gain personal and professional skills that will enable you to co-create positive change in your community. You will also be able to transfer those skills to any environment you encounter in the future, whether in graduate school or during employment. Or perhaps you may be so invested in your community that you will decide to stay and build relationships for just a little while longer—you never know what the future holds.

DEMOGRAPHIC PROFILE

Provide demographic information to complete a community inventory that helps you understand more about your internship community.	

1. Demographics:	a. Population size and rural, urban, suburban b. Income levels c. Poverty rates d. Education levels e. Unemployment rates f. Birth rates g. Infant mortality rates Age distribution h. Racial/Ethnic group distribution *Resources:* www.census.gov www.liveunited.org
2. What trends do you see in the community you are/want to go into? What problems or solutions exist?	a. What barriers prevent problems from being solved? b. What allies exist to help?

3. How can the demographic information help you? Keep in mind that communities can consist of geographic place, age, race/ethnicity, education, etc.

4. Is there something else you could learn that would help you engage with the community you described?

REFERENCES

Anderson, A.A. & Milligan, S. (2006). Social capital and community building. In: Fulbright-Anderson, K. & Auspos, P. (Eds.) *Community change: Theories, practice and evidence.* (21–60). Washington, D.C.: The Aspen Institute.

Anderson, S. A. & Sabatelli, R. M. (2010). *Family Interaction: A Multigenerational Developmental Perspective,* 5th *Ed.* Boston: Allyn and Bacon.

Boeder, P. (2002). Non-profits on E: How Non Profit organisations are using the internet for communication, fundraising, and community building, *First Monday,* 7(7), 1–36.

Duncan, S. F. & Goddard, H. W. (2011) *Family life education: Principles and practices for effective outreach* (2nd ed.)Thousand Oaks, CA: Sage.

Ebersole, M., and Worster, A. (2007). Sense of place in teacher preparation courses: Placebased and standardsbased education. *The Delta Gamma Bulletin* 73(2): 19–24.

Hall, M. (2010). Life map activity. *In Readings for diversity and social justice* (Chapter 1). Retrieved from http://cw.routledge.com/textbooks/readingsfordiversity/section3/ch-01-c.pdf

Maslow, A. H. (1968). Toward a psychology of being. *New York: John.*

Okubo, D., & Weidman, K. (2000). Engaging the community in core public health functions. *National Civic Review, 89*(4), 309–326.

Project Implicit. (2011). https://implicit.harvard.edu/implicit/takeatest.html

Shiraev, E. & Levy, D.A. (2010). *Cross-cultural psychology: Critical thinking and contemporary applications,* 4th Ed. Boston: Allyn and Bacon.

Singer, J. A., King, L. A., Green, M. C., & Barr, S. C. (2002). Personal identity and civic responsibility: "Rising to the occasion" narratives and generativity in community action student interns. *Journal of Social Issues, 58*(3), 535–556.

Slick, G.A. (2000) *Communication: The key to successful field experiences,* Thousand Oaks, CA: Corwin Press.

10 Re-Routing Your GPS

OBJECTIVES

By the end of this chapter you should be able to:

➤ Reflect on your internship
➤ Develop a project
➤ Develop a portfolio
➤ Evaluate your internship experience
➤ Develop a plan for the future

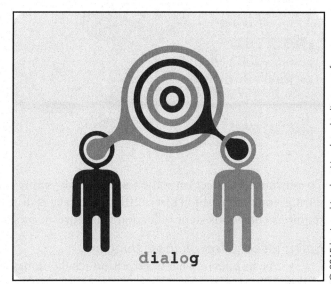

At this point, you are probably in the midst of your internship. It is important that you take the time to constantly reflect on your experience throughout your internship, and that you intentionally document your experience. As you reflect, you think critically about the application of your course knowledge, as well as your interactions with people and places.

During internships, students often report feeling disconnected from their university (Bulger, 2006; Wilkinson, 2008). Due to the fact that a majority of internships are located off-campus and you may or may not have other course responsibilities, maintaining a virtual connection through reflections can provide the opportunity for others to support you, as well as for you to learn from others' experiences.

To avoid feelings of isolation in your internship, you should communicate with your university supervisor and peers throughout your experience. Maintaining contact with your university community is also important to ensure that your internship experience is as useful as possible (Wilkinson, 2008), not only to have the opportunity to describe how your course knowledge is playing out in the real world, but also to actively reflect on your experience (Wilkinson, 2008). Remember our discussion of Kolb's Learning Theory (Kolb, Boyatzis & Mainemelis, 2001)? Being an active participant in your experience will bring it life and enable you to learn meaningfully from your experience.

According to research, your peers in internships appreciate the opportunities to not only reflect on their experience, but also to learn about others (Mayer, 2002). In addition, if you have questions about things occurring in your internship, you can get peer feedback from students in similar placements. At the end of the day, we know that although we, as instructors, can provide the same information, you would much rather hear it from your peers—they are actually living the experience at the same time that you are, not us.

If your university supervisor is planning to use an online discussion platform, it is a useful method of maintaining the connection. If not, you and your peers can use other methods. Although we utilize an online platform in our department, our students often use additional tools as well. Commonly, they form Facebook groups or Group Me for text messages. Look for what works best for you, and make sure that you are reflecting consistently in order to truly make the most of your experience.

OPPORTUNITIES FOR REFLECTION

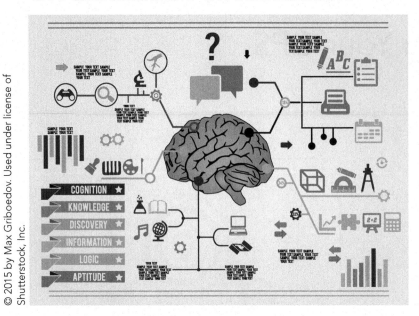

In our department, students complete reflections bimonthly, alternating between specific prompts and peer responses. Your department may have its own guidelines, but here are some ideas for you to consider throughout your internship. Remember key things as you reflect, including confidentiality. Provide enough information to get your point across, but be mindful of the sensitive and personal nature of your reflections; it is necessary to follow all guidelines regarding confidentiality. As you reflect, we also recommend keeping track of your weekly and cumulative hours to ensure that you are completing enough hours to satisfy your internship requirements.

To get started, reflect on some things weekly, while others are things you can think about at some point during your internship (Kiser, 2012; Sweitzer & King, 2009). Remember, regardless of your university requirements, consistent reflection is important to success.

Every week reflect on these things:
- As an intern, what is surprising, challenging, and exciting?
- What has met your expectations?
- What has not met your expectations?
- What have you accomplished?
- What time do you have allocated to meet with your supervisor? How have these meetings been helpful?
- What have you learned from your colleagues?
- What have you learned from the clients?
- What have you learned about the community?
- How have you applied course knowledge?
- How can you use this experience in the future?

At some point during your internship, you should reflect on these things:
- Review your Goals
- How did your goal planning help you in your internship?
- Review your personal, professional and civic goals; how have your personal, professional and civic identities impacted your experiences in the internship?
- Review your strengths, weaknesses, opportunities and threats assessment. How have these changed?
- In what ways have you been a leader? Refer to the community chapter when we discussed leadership.
- Review your goals. Describe how you have made progress towards completing them.
- Use your CFLE Matrix that you used during goal development and briefly describe what you have observed and experienced. Attach or describe the matrix.

Refer to the content on Communication
- What communication styles do your supervisor and coworkers use?
- Have you noticed any generational differences? Explain.

- How have you communicated with clients?
- How have you communicated with the public?
- Identify at least one positive and one negative aspect of your communication.
- How have you communicated with your peers?

Review Ethical Decision Making
- What examples of ethical dilemmas and decisions have you experienced?
- What happens if they are professional standards are violated, both in your agency and society?

Review the Demographic Profile
- Discuss how this information has impacted your experience in your internship.
- Has your knowledge and/or understanding changed?
- Have your perceptions been challenged?
- How has your community membership evolved?

Review your Agency Research
- Ask for agency guidelines if they were not previously given to you, and list and explain at least two policies that are important to you as an intern. Identify other things that you still need to know or learn in order to be successful.
- Describe what you have learned about how your agency operates (non-profit, business, government office, etc.).
- Describe the population that your organization serves and their involvement in the community.
- What are the assets and needs of those served?
- Give basic information about the community they live in.
- How does your project address a community need?
- Agencies are often affiliated with or accredited by National/Professional Organizations, e.g. National Council on Family Relations, American Association of Marriage and Family Therapy, Child Life Council, etc. What National/Professional Organization does your agency belong to, or should belong to?

Challenges
- What issues have arisen that challenged you throughout your internship experience?
- Do they involve people in the community, the agency, or you?
- What has happened this week that has challenged you?
- Discuss how you have addressed these challenges this week or throughout the internship.

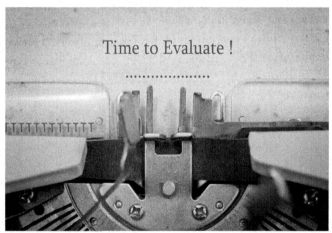

During your internship, we recommend that you complete a midterm and final evaluation of your experience (O'Malley and Wilson, n.d.). Your completion of the evaluation will not only provide future students with information about the types and quality of learning experiences that are available at your internship site, but will also allow you to have a voice during your experience as you reflect on your internship. We encourage you to share your feedback with your supervisor. Supervisors should also complete a midterm and final evaluation of your performance. For both parties, it is a good learning experience to share constructive feedback, as well as receive it. In our department, supervisor evaluations of students account for a percentage of their grade, so we use the information in the Internship Agreement (from Chapter 4) to clearly state what the expectations are of interns. These criteria are then evaluated on the evaluations. Ideas for the content to include in student and supervisor evaluations is included in Appendix A and B.

We also advise that you schedule an exit interview with your supervisor (Bulger, 2006; O'Malley & Wilson, n.d.; Sweitzer & King, 2009). This provides one last opportunity for you to have a dialogue with your site supervisor about the overall experience, and gain his or her perspective on what you can do next given your experiences. Additionally, we encourage you to share your overall experience with your university supervisor and peers. In our department, we utilize our final exam period to allow students to present their projects and experiences to each other so that students learn about the diversity of internships, and see the potential for their futures.

PROPOSING A PROJECT IN YOUR PLACEMENT

Objective: By proposing a project, you will not only continue to explore who you are, but you will also learn about others and your community. This assignment will enable you to think ahead and intentionally choose a project that meets the needs of the community and think about how it directly relates to your learning goals. Complete this assignment after you have an internship. You may know your responsibilities, but not necessarily what your day-to-day tasks will be, so review your goals and brainstorm ideas that will help you accomplish those.

This may be something your internship supervisor assigns you, or you may have to take the initiative and create your own. Regardless, you should get approval for the project from your internship supervisor and your university supervisor. According to The National Council on Family Relations (Hennon, n.d.), there are two types of projects: organization problems or creative, student-initated ideas. A project addressing an organization problem is not necessarily negative. Your supervisor may ask you to develop a new assessment or handbook. This is identified as a need that you can assist the agency with. If there is not a specific issue, then brainstorm to identify a creative project. Examples are provided below.

Problem-Oriented	Student Initiated
Educational pamphlet	Case Study of Clients
Directory of agency resources	Parenting Curriculum
Internship/Volunteer Handbook	Compiling information from interviews conducted with similar agencies to compare procedures
Educational newsletter series	Conducting research on a topic relevant to placement
Web development related to educational programming or service delivery	Creating a handbook of activities, e.g. OT/PT exercises, lesson plans, etc.
Press releases or articles	Conducting a needs assessment
Summary of presentation to staff or families	Compiling a portfolio of multiple mini-projects
Program development, implementation, and/or evaluation	Developing virtual materials to conduct outreach

Now that you have some examples, think outside of the box. What type of project(s) could you do in your internship? Complete the *Proposing a Project* activity in the *Applying Your Knowledge* section of this chapter. Once you have completed that, you can work towards the *Project Action Plan.*

FROM INTERNSHIP TO CAREER

At the end of your internship, you may feel emotional. You may be sad to leave your colleagues and clients that you have established relationships with during your experience. You may also be excited to move on to the next phase in your life. Regardless of what you feel, it is important that you know that these feelings are *normal* (Kiser, 2012). You need to be prepared to leave your internship, the people and the places you have developed a community with over the course of the semester. As you complete your internship, you will need to say goodbye—savor the experience. As you take your next steps, make sure that you leave your mark at your agency, and make an impression so deep that your colleagues want you to stay or recommend you. A number of our students receive offers of part- or full-time employment at the end of the internships, and some even receive correspondence months later requesting that they apply for an open position. You never know what the future may hold, so you need to be clear about your exit. One thing we do not recommend is taking on too much at the end. You want to make it a smooth transition for everyone, so do not leave tasks unfinished.

Before you leave, develop a plan of action for your future. Because most students complete an internship that is directly relevant to their future field, utilize your colleagues and peers during your internship. Ask them to review your resume before you finalize your portfolio. As individuals who review employment applications, they know what they want to see, so take advantage of their knowledge and expertise. Remember that they went through this process with you, sharing their knowledge and passion for the field with you. You need to acknowledge this and say thank you. Express your feelings to your supervisor to let them know how much of an impact they had on your experiences and future.

What professional path did they take to obtain their job?

What level of education do they have; from what school?

Who do they know in the field that you can contact?

At the end of your experience, assess what you have learned. Use the reflective paper as a starting point to think about what this experience has meant, and will mean moving forward. As a final exercise, think about your experience in this internship and write a reflective paper. Additional guidelines are in the *Applying Your Knowledge* section of this chapter.

As you reflect on your experience, we recommend thinking intentionally about your future and completing tasks that will prepare you for it, whether you intend to take a gap year, apply or attend graduate school, or apply for a job. To get started, visualize your future. Resurrect your *Life Map* and depict your life two years into the future.

To understand more about your options, we recommend researching occupations by completing an Occupational Outlook Assessment. You can find this in the *Applying Your Knowledge* section of this chapter.

If you intend to take a gap year, we recommend that you assess your professional options.

1. Review the results of your Occupational Outlook Assessment to determine how you want to gain more experience.
2. Use your university's career center for resources on possible gap year programs, e.g. Teaching English as a Foreign Language Abroad and Teach for America.
3. Explore internship, volunteer or employment options that can provide you with applicable experience.

If you see graduate school in your future, we recommend that you research schools.

1. Decide what region(s) you are interested in residing.
2. Explore the degrees offered at the institution
3. Find a department that fits your interests and assess the content of the courses offered.
4. Browse the faculty list to determine their research or practice areas.
5. Communicate with faculty and current graduate students.
6. Assess whether or not the school and department meet your "Goodness of Fit" criteria.
7. Develop your personal statement letter and get feedback from mentors.
8. Be mindful of timelines regarding the GRE, letters of recommendation and application due dates.

If you intend to apply for a job, we recommend that you prepare yourself for the job market.

1. Begin with a location – assess the job market through the Chamber of Commerce.
2. Use your network and ask about available opportunities in your desired field.
3. Use the internet as a *resource*, but not as the primary tool for your search. We recommend Idealist and USA Jobs and United Way as places to start.
4. Once you have identified options, conduct research.
   a. Explore the organization's LinkedIn or other Social Media platforms.
   b. Explore the employee's LinkedIn Profiles.
5. Compile the necessary documents and apply for the job.
6. Look at the cost of living for the city, state. There are numerous online calculators, so find the one that works best for you. Use this information as you negotiate (always negotiate) a salary should you receive an offer.

DEVELOPING A PORTFOLIO

Regardless of your path, we encourage you to develop your LinkedIn Profile to showcases the work you have completed over the course of the internship and demonstrates experience and value in the field. Developing a profile can be a great way to provide the information to not only your university supervisor and site supervisor, but to future employers as well.

RESUME

Update your resume to include your internship experience, education, and other relevant information.

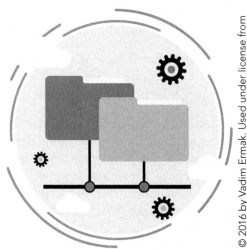

- If you list relevant course work on your resume, provide specific examples of projects, research, or papers that demonstrate why that course is relevant for the job.

- Describe volunteer work in-depth so it is clear what your responsibilities included.
- Include Professional Organization Affiliations
- Include new skills, evidence of work, e.g. grants, public relations material, lesson plans, client care plans, fact sheets, and administrative reports.

You can only provide so much information in a resume, but you can really tell your story using LinkedIn. To use LinkedIn effectively, they recommend that new graduates complete the following tasks (Garriott, 2015; n.a., n.d.)

1. Select an appropriate, professional photograph
2. Write an engaging objective, or headline
3. Provide a representative and concise summary
4. Include all of your employment experiences
5. Create *additional profile* sections to explain your experiences in *Organizations, Education, Volunteerism* and *Honors and Awards, Courses and Projects.*
6. Build your LinkedIn network
7. Claim your unique URL
8. Upload examples of your work
9. Use keywords in the skills section
10. Use LinkedIn's content and learn more

To address number eight on this list, we think it is important for you to compile representative work that demonstrates your knowledge in the field. Review your departmental objectives, course objectives from the *most relevant* courses you have completed, or review the CFLE Competencies and Matrix and identify examples of your best work that demonstrate your knowledge. Appropriate examples can include research papers, case studies, program curriculum, lesson plans, or presentations. Once you have identified relevant work, upload them to your LinkedIn Profile.

PROPOSING A PROJECT

1. Briefly summarize your goals and objectives during your internship. You can refer to the activities from Chapter 4, or your departmental internship application.

Your goals/objectives:

2. Review your demographic survey/perspectives.
3. Review the list of problem-oriented or student-initiated project ideas. Record at least *two ideas* **(they do not have to come from the text ideas)** that you have about a project. For each idea:
   a. List the relevant *Family Life Education Competencies* (p. 27) & **Content areas** (p. 29; p. 76).
   b. Identify how it meets your goals/objectives.
   c. Identify how it meets a community need.
   d. Identify the type of role/approach that your project represents (p. 73).

Project Idea	Competencies	Content Areas	Goal/Objective	Community Need	FLE Role(s)
Ex. Curriculum for parenting program	*Planning & Organization, Writing & Material Development*	**Parent Education and Guidance Human Growth and Development**	I want to learn how to develop curriculum and engage directly with parents.	High rates of abuse/neglect	Facilitator Interventionist

Project Action Plan

Develop a tentative list of options and a plan of action for your internship project. Remember to make this project something beneficial for your future and integrate it into your internship.

1. What project will you complete during your internship?

2. In one sentence, what is your goal with your project? How will you incorporate the project into your responsibilities while working at your internship?

3. Identify the stakeholders (supervisor, colleagues, peers, clients, etc.) and what role they play in your project, particularly looking at what benefit they will receive.

4. What resources do you need to implement the project? Identify the steps you need to take now and during your internship to complete your project (include dialogue with your supervisor).

5. What challenges could you encounter in completing your project? How will you address these?

Reflection Paper

Before completing a formal reflection, take the time to record some initial thoughts about your internship experience.

1. In the first weeks, what do/did you wish you had known?
   a. About the agency

   b. Your responsibilities

2. What would have helped you be successful?

3. What did you learn from your placement?

4. Identify short-term (1 year) and long-term (5 year) goals based on your perceptions and experiences in this internship.

5. Work on (and include) a draft of the thank you letter that we encourage you to provide in your portfolio to your supervisor/agency.

Additional questions to consider
Did you enjoy the population you worked with during your experience? Did you enjoy the agency environment? Why or why not? What aspects of the field are you still interested in exploring? What aspects of the field are you no longer interested in exploring? Where do you see yourself fitting in for your career? Use these questions to critically reflect on your experience and create a plan that coincides with your one- and five-year goals. What path will you choose to travel next?

Occupational Career Assessment

You will use O*Net OnLine (https://www.onetonline.org) to explore your career choice.

1. Select *Find Occupations* and select *Career Cluster* select the most appropriate career field.
2. Select an occupation to learn more.
   A. Occupational title: _____
   B. List other job titles fit into this occupation.

1.
2.
3.
4.
5.

   C. Identify two tasks associated with this occupation.

1.
2.

   D. Identify two skills associated with this occupation.

1.
2.

   E. Identify the education needed:
      _____Certificate _____ AA/AS _____BA/BS _____MA/MS
      _____Doctorate/Professional degree

   F. Identify any other necessary credentials and professional organization memberships.

   G. Identify Salary Information:

	Median (Yearly) Salary
Current Residing State	
Future Residing State (if different from current)	
United States	

   H. Occupational Outlook:

	Projected Job Growth
United States	
	Projected Job Growth
State of Residence/Choice	

   I. Is the outlook/job growth in Georgia (or state of choice) at least average?
      ___Yes ___No

   J. Use a Cost of Living Calculator. Does the salary allow you to meet your needs?
      ___Yes ___No

REFERENCES

Bulger, S. M. (2006). Maintaining Connections: A Web-Enhanced Approach To Undergraduate Internship Supervision. *Physical Educator, 63*(3), 114.

Garriott, O. (2015, February 6). 10 *LinkedIn tips for students & new grads.* Retrieved from https://www.linkedin.com/pulse/10-tips-students-new-grads-linkedin-omar-garriott

George, J.L. (2016) Occupational Career Assessment [Class Activity]. Department of Human Development and Family Science, University of Georgia, Athens, GA.

Hennon, C. (n.d.). Examples of integrated field experience & family life education class. In O'Malley, A.J. & Wilson, J.D. (Eds.) *Pathways to practice: A Family life education internship/practicum handbook.* (J1-29). Minneapolis, MN: National Council on Family Relations.

Kiser, P.M. (2012). The *Human Services Internship:* Getting *The Most From Your Experience* (3rd Ed.). Belmont, CA: Brooks-Cole Publishing.

Kolb, D. A., Boyatzis, R. E. and Mainemelis, C. 2001. Experiential learning theory: Previous research and new directions. *Perspectives on Thinking, Learning, and Cognitive Styles, 1,* 227–247.

Mayer, D. (2002). An Electronic lifeline: Information and Communication Technologies in a Teacher Education Internship. *Asia-Pacific Journal of Teacher Education 30(2),* 181–189.

N.A. (n.d). *LinkedIn Profile Checklist.* Retrieved from https://university.linkedin.com/content/dam/university/global/en_US/site/pdf/LinkedIn_Sample_Profile_onesheet-David.pdf

Sweitzer, H. F., & King, M. A. (2009). The *Successful Internship:* Personal, *Professional,* and *Civic Development* (3rd ed.). Belmont, CA: Brooks-Cole Publishing.

Wilkinson, K. (2008). Using breeze for communication and assessment of internships: An Exploratory study. *Journal of Educators Online, 5*(2), n2.

O'Malley, A. J. and Wilson, J.D. (n.d.) Working Together And Introduction To The Practicum. In The National Council On Family Relations (Eds.), *Pathways to Practice A Family Life Education Internship/Practicum Handbook.* (pp. 2–12). Minnesota: NCFR.

Textbook Bio

JENNIFER L. GONYEA

Dr. Gonyea is a Senior Lecturer in the Human Development and Family Science Department at the University of Georgia. Her teaching focuses on couple and family relationships, family intervention, and professionalism. Dr. Gonyea researches technology and relationships, ethical decision-making, and couple and family therapy. She also engages in the Scholarship of Teaching and Learning and has been selected as both an Online Learning Fellow and a Writing Fellow.

Dr. Gonyea is a Licensed Marriage and Family Therapist and a Licensed Professional Counselor, serving couples and families in crisis through her part-time practice. She is a leader in her profession having served as the President of the Georgia Division of the American Association of Marriage and Family Therapy (AAMFT), the Director of Undergraduate Curriculum, and ans Assistant Editor of the International Journal of Teaching and Learning in Higher Education.

In her spare time, she writes textbooks, prepares TEDx Talks, stand-up paddle boards, geocaches, and seeks adventure near and far with her family.

MELISSA SCOTT KOZAK

Dr. Kozak is a Lecturer and Undergraduate Program Coordinator in the Human Development and Family Science Department at the University of Georgia. Her teaching focuses on human sexuality, family life education, and professionalism. Dr. Kozak the Scholarship of Teaching and Learning to assess effective pedagogical strategies and has been selected as a Writing Fellow.

Dr. Kozak is a Certified Family Life Educator and works with Athens Farm to School to develop children's programming at a local farmers market.

In her spare time, Dr. Kozak writes textbooks and spends time with her husband and son learning about love and life. Most of the year, she can be found at the farmers market, or working with her friends on their farm.

Drs. Gonyea and Kozak have co-developed an internship program aimed toward scaffolding students into their professional identities. The program focuses on experiential learning in a three-course series through self-assessment, applied projects, and community-based placements.

CPSIA information can be obtained
at www.ICGtesting.com
Printed in the USA
LVOW01s1105070716

495254LV00003B/17/P